W9-COB-314

PRAYER POWER

by

Dr. George M. Brown
Distinguished Service Professor
Miami-Dade Community College

PUBLISHED BY

Star Bible Publications
Fort Worth, Texas 76182

PRAYER POWER

Copyright © 1992 by Star Bible Publications, Inc.
Fort Worth, Texas 76182

Cover Credit: Hands of Power were carved and photographed by Stephen H. Prescott. The hands are on display in the Garden of Prayer, North Richland Hills, Texas. The garden is a project of the Prayer Awareness Ministry, Church of Christ. Alvin Jennings, chairman.

All rights reserved. No portion of this book may be reproduced in any form without the written permission of the Publisher.

Printed in the United States of America.

ISBN 0-940999-94-3

TABLE OF CONTENTS

Dedication

Beverly & Charles Gatton

In the heart of a city in the heart of America is a congregation of the church of Christ dedicated to helping the poor. It has now been 30 years since my wife and I were serving a brief tour in a slum area to establish the work of the Lord. Then, at a time when the sponsoring elders were ready to close the doors, Charles and Beverly Gatton suggested that we could make a go of the work if we were to stay there and they would join us. With the elders' permission, we did "make a go" of the work. We asked others to join us. With their help, we managed to rescue hundreds of the downtrodden. To this day, the

Downtown church of Christ in Kansas City, Missouri, continues to serve the needy in that area and to send its clarion call that the Lord will bless such efforts.

Charles and Beverly Gatton have been truly saints of the Lord throughout the time I have known them -- truly caring about the needs of others. In many ways, they have provided direct support for a ministry I have undertaken on behalf of abused/abandoned children, including paying for my wife's salary for the past seven years. My gratitude knows no bounds.

This book is a gift of love, as was the work in the slum area begun 30 years ago. It is given on behalf of the needy. And to the ones who were so vital to the original dream -- Charles and Beverly Gatton, this book is gratefully dedicated. Surely, when the Lord comes again to claim his own, they'll reign with him forever ever more.

...and Appreciation

If ever a woman deserved the description of Proverbs 31, it is my wife, Barbara. For her price is indeed far above rubies! She has never hesitated a step to follow wherever I would lead. She went without a murmur into a slum area to serve the poor in Kansas City. She has cared for the children who needed a home. (And I never once heard her complain or refuse my request.) She has allowed me the time to counsel and otherwise minister to others. She has trained three lovely daughters in the nurture and admonition of the Lord. She has served as a teacher and as an administrator for Christian causes. Her life is so filled with virtue, not only her family but all who know her rise up and call her "blessed."

Warning

You may read all of the books ever written about prayer, but until you actually choose -- with heart, mind and soul -- to pray, you will never learn. Do not, therefore, expect to profit from reading this book on *Prayer Power* until you personally enter into the real classroom of prayer -- Your closet!

As you struggle to pray, you will, however, probably not learn to pray powerfully until you have been taught. If my forty-five years on the Lord's church is typical, you will have received very little instruction on prayer. Fewer than fifteen sermons devoted exclusively to instruction in prayer have been preached in my hearing. This book is, therefore, designed to close this vital gap.

The Bible is the book for teaching the believer to pray. Yet, because instruction regarding prayer is often widely scattered throughout scripture, this book attempts to bring precept and practice regarding prayer together into one place that each of us may "come boldly before the throne of grace"[1] "lifting up holy hands without wrath and doubting."

Let the mediation of every searcher's heart be: "Lord, teach me to pray."[2] In other words, pray to learn and learn to pray.

Chapter I

PRAYER POWER REALLY WORKS

> "Lord, I believe; help thou mine unbelief."
> -Mark 9:24

A Cloud of Witnesses

"It's only 37 minutes from Moscow to New York. And only 37 minutes from New York to Moscow." The casual listener might think the speaker was referring to some mode of transportation -- perhaps, some time in the distant future. Yet, this was a general of the United States military stating the amount of time for a nuclear warhead to strike from the most prominent cities in Russia and in the United States.

Even as nations store up fire, the destructive force of atomic bombs is almost incomprehensible. Yet, many prominent persons have claimed even greater power from prayer. The late J. Edgar Hoover, director of the F.B.I., has stated:

> *"The spectacle of a nation praying is more awe-inspiring than the explosion of an atomic bomb. The force of prayer is greater than any possible combination of man-made or man-controlled powers, because prayer is man's greatest means of tapping the infinite resources of God. Invoking by prayer the mercy and might of God is our most efficacious means of guaranteeing peace and security for the harassed and helpless peoples of the earth."*[1]

Isaac Newton, one of the greatest scientists who ever lived, also attested to the power of prayer:

> *"I can take my telescope and look millions and millions of miles into space; but I can lay my telescope aside, go into my room and shut the door, get down on my knees in earnest prayer, and I see more of heaven and get closer to God than I can when assisted by all the telescopes and material agencies on earth."*[2]

Yet, perhaps, Eliza M. Hickok said it best in her verse, "He Answers":

> *"I know not by what methods rare,*
> *But this I know, God answers prayer.*
> *I know not when He sends the word*
> *That tells us fervent prayer is heard*
> *I know it cometh soon or late;*
> *Therefore we need to pray and wait.*
> *I know not if the blessing sought*
> *Will come in just the guise I thought.*
> *I leave my prayers with Him alone*
> *Whose will is wiser than my own."*[3]

According to a recent Gallop Poll, 88% of Americans engage in prayer to God:

> 96% to "thank God for his blessings."
> 91% to "ask God to forgive their sins."
> 90% to "ask God for guidance."
> 70% to "try to listen to God speaking to you."
> 68% to " spend time adoring God."
> 42% to "ask God for material things."[4]

Despite the claims, can it really be demonstrated that prayer power really works?

Does Prayer Power Really Work?

Ask the man who fled for his life "in great fear and distress,"[5] from his sworn enemy who lived "by the sword."[6] Having exhausted all avenues of escape humanly possible, he turned to the Lord God and prayed, "Save me."[7]

Yet, what did he see when he awoke the next morning? Four hundred men, armed to the teeth, coming directly toward him. ("Some answer to prayer," he must have thought.) Yet, they parted before him until at last he faced his dreaded foe, who he knew would kill him. However, as his enemy raced toward him, "embraced him, fell on his neck, and kissed him... and as they wept together...,"[8] he knew that the Lord God really does answer prayer.

Ask the man before that day, "What is your name?" He would answer "Jacob." And so, after that night of his having agonized in prayer, he would for the rest of his life be called "Israel" because he had "wrestled"[9] with God and "prevailed."[10]

Inquire of the man who said, "Pray for me:

"...to take away these frogs."[11]
"...that the swarms of flies may depart."[12]
"...that there be no more hail"[13]
"...take away from me this death only." (the locusts)[14]

Upon each occasion of his asking, he saw the prevailing power of prayer for himself and for his people.

The prayer of that righteous man availed much -- the frogs all were killed,[15] all of the flies were removed,[16] the hail ceased,[17] every locust was taken away.[18]

Yet, despite having witnessed wonders *few* have ever seen in their lifetime, he was to witness one more wonder.

"Don't pray for me any more"?[19] he told the man of God. Yet, when the "loud wailing" was heard -- "worse than there ever has been or ever will be again"[20] -- since the first-born of every man and every beast would die, he would join the chorus of wailers as his own first-born son would die.

Does not, even now the voice of Pharaoh of Egypt, cry out, as it were, from the grave, "Prayer power really works. If only I had asked for prayer one more time...!"

Question the woman who mumbled and moaned, who behaved so strangely a man of God accused her of being drunk. Ask the barren Hannah how she not only could conceive a child but also predetermine the sex of the child.[21] Let the mother of Samuel, the greatest judge of Israel and one of the greatest prophets who ever lived sing her prayer song so eloquently that it turns to prophecy. In I Samuel 2, read in every joyous sentence, "Prayer power really works."

Examine the woman who learned that a bribe was being collected for the purpose of exterminating an entire race of people. Learn how it felt as perhaps $3,000,000 were being collected. Realize how she, armed only with prayer and fasting, walked into the king's throne room unannounced. Walk with her as she faced death if the king did not raise his scepter. Understand how her request to spare the lives of a nation was granted. Does not the entire book of Esther proclaim most eloquently, "Prayer power really works."[22]

Meet the man born a slave, a nobody, who lived with one passion: to be free -- to go home again -- to worship in freedom. Let the man who, when his master finally set him free, tell that he was too ashamed to ask for an armed escort.[23] "Can the free people stand the sight of so many slaves leaving--never to return?" Yet, he would go-- armed only with prayer and fasting.[24] Accompany Ezra, as he and his fellow slaves survived the perilous journey, how they came to worship as a free people in their own house of worship. Do we not hear the echo of their freedom shout, "Prayer power really works!"

Come to the bedside of a man who lay dying -- in shame and disgrace. He had also just lost the war. Only one more battle to be fought and all would be over. Stay by that bedside and learn how the tide battle was turned -- how the death sentence was lifted by a single prayer. Meet Hezekiah, king of Judah, and learn the most significant lesson he ever learned, "Prayer power really works."[25]

Suddenly, find yourself in an ancient city and there visit a man who has just been awakened in the night to see the entire city surrounded with enemy soldiers and chariots. Fearing for his life, he asked his master, "What shall we do?" Imagine the absolute bewilderment in the answer to do nothing. It has already been done. The prayer for deliverance has already been given. Hear the man of God say:

> *"Lord I pray thee, open his eyes that he may see."*[26]

Look about and see what the servant saw -- the army of the enemy struck blind and behold an even greater army of horses and chariots of fire surrounding them. Go with that now-shameful servant and the prophet Elisha as they lead and feed their once fierce foe back toward their land never to attack again. Can you not hear Elisha as well as his servant -- rise in grateful chorus, "Prayer power really works."

Picture the man at the altar praying for a son. Suddenly an angel appears and announces, "Your prayer is heard."[27] Here was a priest from the country who had one chance in a lifetime to serve in the big city for a period of six months. And so, there he was at the altar with the people outside the temple as he performed the divine service. Was it wrong for him somehow to weave into his prayers for all of the people one private, personal petition? The Lord God did not think so, for he sent a very special angel to announce the good news. The man and his wife were going to have a son. His immediate thought was, "I don't believe it." But the angel announced,

> *"I am Gabriel, that stands in the presence of God; and am sent to speak unto thee, and to show thee these glad tidings. And, behold, thou shalt be dumb, and not able to speak, until the day that these things shall be performed, because thou believest not my words, which shall be fulfilled in their season."*[28]

Consider the enormity of the curse given to the man. If, as can be supposed, the angel's visit came in the middle of the six-month period of ministration, then he had to return home and be with his wife from conception through delivery, the period of time he could not speak was probably about a year. Yet, whatever curse, whatever time to wait, it was well worth it. For not only did Zacharias and Elizabeth "have joy and gladness," the world would also "rejoice at his birth."[29] For, as Jesus Christ would declare of him, "among them that are born of women there hath not risen a greater than John the

Baptist...."[30] If Zacharias could but speak to us even now would he not shout, "Prayer power really works."

She answered the knock at the door, but she was so happy to see the would-be guest she didn't even let him in. She ran to tell the others who were at that very moment praying for the man's release from prison. When she told them the good news, that their prayers had been answered, they told her, "You're out of your mind."[31] But when he continued knocking and pray-ers came to the door, they still could hardly believe. Yet, does not the thrilling story of the release of Simon Peter from prison give us pause to reflect upon our own doubts? Does not the answer to the disbelieving Rhoda and to the other doubting Christians knock most loudly at the door of each heart, "Prayer power really works."

Five Challenges

Dear reader, if as has been claimed, prayer power really does works, the best way for you to *begin* to discover the manifold riches of His grace is to put it to the test. Accordingly, you may use the following five scripture-based challenges to the Christian heart.

I.   **Help somebody who cannot help him/herself! Help a homeless child or an aged widow.** James 1:27 reminds believers, *"Pure religion and undefiled before God and the Father is this, To visit the fatherless and widows in their afflictions...."*

II. **Enjoy the fullest measure of the fruit of the Spirit!** Many Christians drag through life "satisfied" with less than the best. Notice the blessed assurance of Isaiah 26:3: "Thou wilt keep him *in perfect peace* whose mind is stayed on Thee, because he trusts in Thee." The Spanish translation is even more impressive "en completa paz" (in complete peace). Not only is perfect peace *available to every one* of God's born again beautiful[32] but also each of the other aspects of the abundant grace: Paul charged the Galatians, *"Walk in the Spirit."*[33] Then he assures them of the results of that walk "...the fruit of the Spirit is *love, joy, peace, long-suffering, goodness, faith, meekness, temperance*, against such there is no law."[34] How else but through our "conversation" fixed in heaven?[35]

III.   **Do a kind deed every day.** The Apostle Paul urged the Galatians to "do good unto all men, especially unto them who are of the household of faith."[36] Yet, we must not "salute" our brothers only.[37] Rather, our *daily* doing good must include overt acts of kindness for even those we consider enemies. Thus, look for (and you will find) your enemies "hungry" and "thirsty." Feed him and give him drink "...for in so doing thou shalt heap coals of fire upon his head."[38]

IV.   **Give at least 10 percent of your income to the Lord.** Hear the prophet Malachi proclaim the words of the Lord God himself:

"Bring ye all the tithes into the storehouse, that there may be meat in mine house, and prove me herewith, saith the Lord of hosts, if I will not open you the windows of heaven, and pour out a blessing that there shall not be room enough to receive it."[39]

Before dismissing this "offer" as not "binding" upon the church, consider the challenge of Christ:

> *"Woe to you, scribes and Pharisees, hypocrites! for ye pay tithe of mint and anise and cummin, and have omitted the weightier matters of the law, judgment, mercy, and faith; these ought ye to have done and not leave the other undone."*[40]

Does not our master <u>commend</u> tithing (giving 10 percent of one's income) <u>as</u> <u>well</u> <u>as</u> other "weightier matters"? Indeed, Christ challenges us:

> *"Give and it shall be given unto you; good measure, pressed down, and shaken together, and running over, shall men heap into your bosom."*[41]

V.   **Become a soul winner for Jesus.** Can you point to any "fruit" you have brought forth for him?[42] Jesus told his disciples that "the harvest truly is plenteous, but the laborers are few."[43] Then he gave the methodology for soul winning:

> *"Pray ye therefore the Lord of the harvest, that he will send forth laborers into his harvest."*[44]

As you consider these challenges to your Christian heart, plan through prayer to commit to them each day. You will, of course, want to *add* your own challenges. What is needed most of all, it would seem, is a central core of challenges that act as an anchor guiding the pilgrim bark aright. Ben Johnson once wrote words so true: "How ready is heaven to those that pray."[45]

Precious Promises

Of all the "exceeding great and precious promises,"[46] none is more precious than the realization: **PRAYER POWER REALLY WORKS!** The Psalmist penned the words of the Lord God: "Ask of me and I will give you the heathen for an inheritance, and the uttermost parts of the earth for your inheritance."[47] He must have put the Lord to the test, for we later read these words from the Psalmist David himself: "You have delivered me from the strivings of the people, and you have made me the head of the heathen...a people whom I have not known shall serve me."[48]

A recent report of a medical study at San Francisco General Medical Center's coronary care unit in 1982 and 1983 provides evidence of the efficacy of prayer power independent of the scriptures themselves.   A Dr. Randolph Byrd divided 393 patients between a group whose health was prayed for by three to seven born-again Christians and a control group that did not receive such prayers. Patients were not told which group they were in. But those who were prayed for had fewer complications during their stay.   Dr. John Thomison, editor of the *Southern Medical Journal* that published the study, stated, "Prayer is about as benign a form of treatment as there is."[49]

Chapter II

PRAYER POWER UNLIMITED

> "How ready is Heaven to those that pray!"
> -Ben Johnson

Dealing With Doubts

"We must have a watchdog!" And so, the husband, having heard his wife's plea day after day, finally went to the place where watchdogs were sold. The salesman came out with a little Chihuahua. To which the husband replied, "You don't understand. I said I needed a watchdog." The salesman explained, "But you don't understand, Sir. This dog knows karate. All you have to do is to say the word, 'karate,' and tell it what to break. You see that foot-high stack of boards at the end of the counter. 'Karate those boards.'" The little Chihuahua jumped up and went through the boards like a ripsaw. The salesman followed up quickly. "You see that two-foot pile of bricks. 'Karate those bricks.'" And like a knife through butter the dog broke the bricks.

The man was so impressed he bought the dog, took it home and showed it to his wife. "That's no watchdog," she exclaimed. "But, dear, this dog knows karate." "Karate, my foot"!

There will doubtless be some skepticism about that story. As well there should be. Yet, when it comes to assessing the power of prayer, many want to dismiss it, as with the story of the little Chihuahua. The following stories are even more fantastic, beyond *any power known to man*. Yet, each one has verification deep in the roots of history.

"Is anything too hard for the Lord?"[1] the Lord God asked of Abraham. Yet, even as Sarah "laughed within herself" because she and Abraham "were old and well stricken in age, and it ceased to be with Sarah after the manner of women," the Lord promised: "At the time appointed I will return unto thee, according to the time of life, and Sarah shall have a son."[2]

Imagine the impossibility of a child to be born to a couple almost 100 years of age. And so, when the child of promise was born "at the time appointed," the very name they chose, Isaac -- which means laughter -- would forever serve as a reminder of their doubt of the Lord God's ability to "do exceedingly abundantly above all that we ask or think."[3]

The Lord God also challenged Jeremiah, "Is anything too hard for me?"[4] -- immediately after the weeping prophet had declared in fervent prayer:

> *"Ah, Lord God, Thou hast made the heaven and the earth by thy great power and stretched out arm, and there is nothing too hard for Thee."*[5]

With Jeremiah, this was no idle boast for he had already acted according to his conviction. Israel and Judah had already been overrun by the Babylonians under King Nebachadnezzar. Finally, Jerusalem had come under siege. Ultimate collapse was not far off. Even so Zedekiah, King of Judah, did not want to keep on hearing bad news. Hence, he imprisoned the old "windbag."

From his prison cell, Jeremiah summoned his cousin Hanamel and commanded him to buy a field in the territory of Benjamin (already conquered by the Babylonians). He further instructed Hanamel to place copies of the deed in a clay jar that would preserve the deed for a long time. At a time when everybody was being overcome by sword, famine and plague, Jeremiah trusted completely in the word of the Lord God, that the land would one day be restored to the people now being so cruelly cast out. Thus, we can see, Jeremiah was willing to "put his money where his mouth was." And so, Jeremiah lived as he prayed, *"There is nothing too hard for Thee."*[6]

Was it not through *prayers* of faith that the people of the Lord God

> *"...subdued kingdoms, wrought righteousness, obtained promises, stopped the mouths of lions, quenched the violence of fire, escaped the edge of the sword, out of weakness were made strong, waxed valiant in fight, turned to flight the armies of the aliens. Women received their dead raised to life again...."*[7]

Indeed, the scriptures are replete with "so great cloud of witnesses"[8] that the string of "impossible" victories is interrupted only when the Lord's people fail to continue "instant in prayer,"[9] "lifting up holy hands, without wrath and doubting."[10]

"Whatsoever You May Ask."

John devotes more space in his gospel account to one single event than any other gospel record of any single event including the death, burial and resurrection of Jesus. That event is the Last Supper. John's recounting of that sorrowful scene begins with Jesus washing the feet of his disciples in chapter 13 and does not end until the first verse of chapter 18 -- five of the 21 chapters in the gospel of John.

The most frequent reference Jesus makes at the Last Supper is to the power of prayer. Time and again Jesus offers His blessed assurance that there is no limit to the power of prayer.

> *"Whatsoever ye shall ask in my name, that will I do that the Father may be glorified in the Son."*[11]

> *"If ye ask any thing in my name, I will do it."*[12]

> *"If ye abide in me, and my words abide in you, ye shall ask what you will, and it shall be done unto you."*[13]

> *"...that whatsoever ye shall ask of the Father in my name, he may give it you."*[14]

> *"Verily, Verily, I say unto you, whatsoever ye shall ask the Father in my name, he will give it you"*[15]

> *"Ask, and ye shall receive, that your joy may be full."*[16]

Six times altogether, more frequently than in all the rest of the holy scriptures combined, Jesus reassures the grieving group of apostles -- PRAYER POWER HAS NO LIMITS!!

In proffering His most precious promises, Jesus provides only these conditions:

1. Glorification of the Father.

2. Utterances in the name of Jesus.

3. Abidance in the word and will of Jesus.

Jesus gives only one reason for the creator and covenant maker's willingness to be so commanded by His creation:

"... that your joy may be full."[17]

Having made his message complete, Jesus concludes His charge with a question: "Do you now believe"?[18]

Then Jesus practices what He has been preaching: **HE PRAYS!** Though He often prayed all night long, He offers his longest recorded prayer at the Last Supper. It fills the entire seventeenth chapter of John. Matthew and Mark add that, after Jesus' prayer, "When they had sung a hymn, they went out into the Mount of Olives,"[19] where Jesus, the Prince of Pray-ers, wrestled alone in prayer.

Some have objected that Jesus was speaking exclusively to the apostles. Accordingly, the promise of unlimited prayer power was given exclusively to the apostles, and therefore applies only to the miraculous powers that would be given to them. However, John uses the same language when he reiterates the same promise to the church of Christ in a subsequent letter:[20]

"These things have I written unto you that believe on the name of the Son of God; that ye may know that ye have eternal life, and that ye may believe on the name of the Son of God.

*And this is the confidence that we have in Him,
if we ask any thing according to His will, He
heareth us.*

*And if we know that He hear us, whatsoever we
ask, we know that we have the petitions that we
desired of Him."*[21]

Notice that John reiterates precisely the same wonderful words of Jesus:

"whatsoever we ask"[22] and *"if we ask any
thing."*[23]

Can there be any doubt that "there is no restraint to the Lord,"[24] that He has unlimited power and that He will use it to answer the prayers of His children?

Keep Not Silence

"Ye that make mention of the Lord, keep not silence"[25] was the admonition of Isaiah. For the "Lord's hand is not shortened that it cannot save; neither his ear heavy, that it cannot hear."[26]

After Solomon's prayer at the dedication of the temple, the Lord appeared to him by night, assuring him not only that his prayer has been heard but also that the creator and covenant maker could: 1) shut up the heavens that there would be no rain, 2) command locusts to devour the land and 3) send pestilence among "my people." The one sure method of preventing these calamities and causing them to cease was the realization for prevailing prayer. The wisdom stated by the Lord God was:

*"If my people which are called by my name shall
humble themselves, and pray, and seek my face,*

*and turn from their wicked ways: then will I
hear from heaven, and will forgive their sin, and
will heal their land, now mine eyes shall be
open, and mine ears attend unto the prayer that
is made in this place."*[27]

So convinced of the correlation between the physical
calamities occasioned by the sins of Israel that Solomon
supplicated for relief from "famine, pestilence, blasting,
mildew, locust or...whatsoever plague...whatsoever
sickness"[28] before they should come upon the Lord God's
chosen people.

A three-and-one-half year drought came and went
through the prevailing prayers of the great prayer
warrior, Elijah.[29] In his summation, James tells us
plainly:

*"Elias was a man subject to like passions as we
are, and he prayed earnestly that it might not
rain: and it rained not on the earth by the space
of three years and six months. And he prayed
again and the heaven gave rain, and the earth
brought forth her fruit."*[30]

The occasion of the book of Joel was a devastating locust
plague. Hence, when the prophet urges God's people to
avoid the destructive judgment "day of the Lord"[31] to
"rend your heart and not your garments,"[32] his directions
to use prayer power are quite specific:

*"Sanctify ye a feast, call a solemn assembly,
gather the elders and all the inhabitants of the
land into the house of the Lord your God, and
cry unto the Lord...."*[33]

Ezekiel prophesied that a third of God's people would perish of a pestilence and famine.[34]   Jeremiah, in describing the same coming calamity, used the word *pestilence* 17 times. He declared that those who did not go into captivity would die by pestilence. Though neither of these prophets could persuade the people to repent, the scripture in plain that they themselves were spared through prayer power.[35]

During His sermon on the Mount, Jesus encourages the faithful to "ask and it shall be given unto you."[36] Then, when the Lord tells Isaiah, "I am the Lord, and there is none else,"[37]   He challenges that great prophet to "command ye me."[38]

Fellowship Of The Mystery

Our Lord died that He might bring into existence the church of Christ. For as Paul reminded the congregation at Ephesus:

> *"Christ...loved the church and he gave himself for it; that he might sanctify and cleanse it with the washing of water by the word. That He might present it to Himself a glorious church, not having spot or wrinkle, or any such thing, but that it should be holy and without blemish."*[39]

Paul further describes the church as the "fellowship of the mystery,"[40] prevailing in all things pertaining to life and Godliness because of prayer power "working in us."[41]

The early church was a receiving church. They knew constant victory. Consider for example:

"The Lord added to the church daily such as should be saved."[42]

"And believers were the more added to the Lord, multitudes both of men and women."[43]

"And the Word of God increased; and the number of the disciples multiplied in Jerusalem exceedingly; and a great company of the priests were obedient to the faith."[44]

After the establishment of the church of Christ, every chapter of its history as recorded in Acts declares a victory-receiving church.

The early church was a receiving church because they were an asking church.

*"They continued steadfastly in the apostles' teaching and fellowship, in the breaking of bread and **in prayers.**"*[45]

Thus, the early church was a praying church. For prayer is the key that unlocks the storehouse of God wherein are the "unsearchable riches of Christ."[46]

THE BEGINNING = S T O P

The mighty Amazon river begins its flow from a place where even a small child can step across it. So, too, your initial stream of prayers may begin as a trickle but can expand its flow into the eternal "river of water of life."[47]

The public speaker receives good advice that when he comes before his listener to pause before beginning his speech. As one speech professor expressed it, "Learn to start from a stop." In like manner, the pray-er should start "every thing by prayer and supplication with thanksgiving, letting your requests be made known unto God."[48]

How many times have we come to stop signs? In the future, why not let each one take on a special meaning.

Let each letter have its own meaning.

Special
Times
Of
Prayer

At each of life's crossroads, let each believer learn to **S - T - O - P**; for prayer is prelude!

How many times have we undertaken tasks only to fail miserably when we try to "go it alone?" Why not ask the best friend one could ever have to help? "What a friend we have in Jesus!" is not just a song but a way of life!

A group of missionaries-in-training once received a computerized set of difficult problems that would test their ability to function in a strange culture. With the successful completion of each problem, they received points added to their scores. With each failure, they lost points. What they didn't know was that prayer before each task was factored into the score. Those who remembered to pray were the only ones to pass the test. How true to life!

Prayer is prelude to success! Alfred Lord Tennyson has stated, "More things are wrought by prayer than this world dreams of."[49] And Jesus promised, "Therefore, I say unto you, 'What things soever ye desire, when ye pray, believe that ye receive them, and ye shall have them.'"[50]

"Confess your faults one to another,
and pray for one another...."

-James 5:16

"The effectual fervent prayer of a righteous man availeth much."

-James 5:16

(*Dr. George Brown*, author of **Prayer
Power,** has raised over $1,000,000
for abused/abandoned children.)

Chapter III

A HOUSE OF PRAYER

> "My house shall be called the house of prayer."
> -Isaiah 56:7

Setting The Record Straight

Nazi dictator Adolph Hitler "came to Germany from Italy," "invaded Japan," and "died before World War II," according to school compositions of some teen-age dependents of United States military personnel living in Germany. As reported in The Washington Post,[1] many of the students displayed confusion in their compositions about nearly every aspect of Hitler. At best, students showed only a general sort of piece-meal knowledge.

As the wisdom of Solomon warned, "There is no remembrance of former things."[2] Accordingly, as the aged apostle Peter penned, "I think it meet as long as I am in his tabernacle, to stir you up by putting you in remembrance."[3]

Try to recall events in your own life and you, too, may be confused or perhaps not even remember at all. Yet, the word of God warns us that the true history of every person's life is being kept -- stored up until the day when the books will be opened and all persons will be judged according to their works.[4] Indeed, "Every idle word that men shall speak, they shall give account thereof in the day of judgment."[5] Thus, the record will be complete -- nothing will be left out.

There is, however, a way to set the record straight -- to escape the eternal punishment where there is "...fire that never shall be quenched."[6] God's plan is penitent prayer. For just as every idle word is stored up, so too are the prayers of saints. The prophet John saw in the midst of the throne four beasts and twenty-four elders falling down before the Lamb of God having "...golden vials full of odors, which are the prayers of saints."[7]

Prayer can correct the uncorrected. For as Jesus concluded, "By thy words thou shalt be justified, and by thy words thou shalt be condemned."[8] Hence, the need for every child of God who beholds "what manner of love the Father hath bestowed upon us"[9] must be that of the disciples who asked Jesus, "Lord, teach us to pray."[10]

As Jesus conducted instruction in prayer, He took the question to mean, "Lord, teach *me* to pray." For He taught that prayer is a personal and private matter. He condemned long public prayers, while commending by precept and by practice long personal prayers in a private place. "When thou prayest, enter into thy closet, and when thou hast shut thy door, pray to thy Father which is in secret."[11]

Cleanse Your Temple

The "closet" to which Jesus referred is not only a special location but also the very being of the pray-er himself. John describes the first public act of Jesus regarding the nature of worship when he relates:

> *"And the Jew's Passover was at hand, and Jesus went up to Jerusalem, and found in the temple those that sold oxen and sheep and doves, and the changers of money sitting: And when He had made a scourge of small cords, He drove them all out of the Temple, and the sheep and the oxen; and poured out the changers' money, and overthrew the tables; and said to them that sold doves, 'Take these things hence; make not my Father's house a house of merchandise.'"*[12]

Thus, Jesus "cleansed the temple" in that He cleared the way for worship "in spirit and in truth."[13]

As a sign that what He did was God's will, Jesus said, "Destroy this temple, and in three days I will raise it up."[14] It was not until after the resurrection that His very own disciples fully understood. "He spoke of the temple of His body."[15]

Recall that Jesus cleansed the temple at the beginning of His ministry. Subsequently, He preached, prayed and wept over Jerusalem for three years. Then, He came again at the very end of His ministry to the city of David. People outside the city cried, "Hosanna to the Son of David. Blessed is He that cometh in the name of the Lord; Hosanna in the highest."[16] Ironically, He came to a city that still did not know Him. For "all the city was moved, saying, 'Who is this?'" Yet, though the multitude announced that He was "Jesus, the prophet of Nazareth of Galilee," the real character of Him who cometh in the name of the Lord was more insightfully revealed when He once again

> *"... went into the temple of God, and cast out all them that sold and bought in the temple, and overthrew the tables of the moneychangers, and the seats of them that sold doves. And said unto them, 'It is written, my house shall be called the house of prayer.'"*[17]

As Jesus cleansed the temple the second time, He announced the methodology for cleansing: the true believer must himself become a house of prayer. Recall that when Jesus cleansed the temple the first time, He prophesied that if He ("this temple") were destroyed, He would be raised.[18] Accordingly, as Jesus spoke of Himself as a house of prayer, His challenge is the same for every Christian born again of water and of spirit:[19] learn how to become a house of prayer. For as Paul reminded the Corinthians, "Know ye not that ye are the temple of God, and that the spirit of God dwells in you."[20]

Learning How To Behave

Prevailing prayer requires the actuality of perpetual practice, that one may learn how to behave in the house of God, which is the church of the living God.[21] Accordingly, the laborer[22] constructs his house of prayer filled with:

ADORATION: Moses said, "He is our praise."[23] David prayed, "Oh, Lord, our Lord, how excellent is thy name in all the earth."[24] Jesus taught, "Our Father, which art in heaven, Hallowed be thy name."[25] Angels in heaven cry, "Amen: Blessing, and glory, and wisdom, and thanksgiving, and honor, and power and might, be unto our God forever and ever. Amen."[26]

Nathaniel Hawthorne in "The Great Stone Face" tells how one Ernest, as a boy, lived in a village surrounded by mountains. On one of the mountains, a sculptor had etched the face of a man. Ernest, remarkably impressed, looked for the image in the face of every person he met, but to no avail. He grew up and left the village and did not return again until he was an old man. Even then, he did not fail in his quest to find someone who fitted the image. Upon his return to the village, even as he stared in awe at "the great stone face," someone else looked at the face of Ernest and declared, "It's him!" Ernest had become the very essence of the one he admired. Will not others see the face of God reflected through each one who truly adores the true and living God?

CONFESSION: Having seen the King, the Lord of hosts, Isaiah realized, "Woe is me. For I am undone; because I am a man of unclean lips."[27] Having been confronted with his sin, David begged, "Create in me a clean heart, Oh God. Renew a right spirit within me."[28] Having forgiven others -- and only then, the child of God petitions, "Forgive me my debts as I have forgiven others."[29]

"There is none righteous, no, not one."[30] "For all have sinned and come short of the glory of God."[31] Having remained deeply sensitive to his sinful nature and of specific sins,[32] his self-reproach surfaces as confession, having been assured that if we confess our sins, He is faithful and just to forgive us our sins to cleanse us from all unrighteousness."[33] For He beholds our helpless estate "...his compassion fails not."[34]

The Bible admonishes us to confess Christ "before men."[35] At the beginning of the Reformation, one Martin of Bosle came to a knowledge of the truth but was afraid to make public confession. And so, he wrote on a leaf of parchment, "O most merciful Christ, I know that I can be saved only by the merit of thy blood. Holy Jesus, I acknowledge thy sufferings for me. I love thee! I love thee!" Then he removed a stone from the wall of his chamber and hid it there. The inscription remained hidden for more than 100 years. On the other hand, the great reformer, Martin Luther, stated, "My Lord has confessed me before men; I will not shrink from confessing him before men." The world remembers well Martin Luther; but who remembers Martin of Bosle, or who cares? Solomon wrote that even "open rebuke is better than secret love."[36]

THANKSGIVING: David urged, "Forget not all his benefits."[37] Thus, "Enter into His gates with thanksgiving and into His courts with praise."[38] Paul characterizes walking wisely as "giving thanks always for all things (each thing) unto God and the Father in the name of the Lord Jesus Christ,"[39] for "the fruit of our lips" is "giving thanks to His name."[40]

An unknown versifier has encouraged: "In Every Thing Give Thanks."

> "'Mid sunshine, cloud or stormy days,
> When hope abounds or care dismays,
> When trials press and toils increase
> Let not thy faith in God decrease--
> 'In every thing give thanks.'
>
> "All things we know shall work for good,
> Nor would we change them if we could;
> 'Tis well if only He command;
> His promises will ever stand--
> 'In every thing give thanks.'
>
> "He satisfies the longing heart,
> He thwarts the tempter's cruel dart,
> With goodness fills the hungry soul,
> And helps us sing when billows roll.
> 'In every thing give thanks.'"

SUPPLICATION: Paul pleaded with the Ephesian Christians to "put on the whole armor of God," "praying always with all prayer and supplication in the Spirit."[41] James promises the faithful petitioner that "his effectual, fervent prayer" (supplication -- Revised Version) "avails much."[42]

The behavioral construct, or the A C T S of prayer, is of paramount importance: for the Lord who sees in secret will "reward thee openly"[43] -- so that *all* others may see the results. Hence, though one may go to the temple to pray, he must not be thankful in a boastful way -- praying only within himself and feeling good about it. Rather, the pray-er must *begin* as the publican -- throwing himself on the mercy of the heavenly court with the confession that he is a sinner.[44]

The child of God who fixes his every conversation in heaven[45] must learn to labor fervently, actually to agonize, in prayer as did Epaphras for the Colossian Christians to "stand perfect and complete in all the will of God."[46] Accordingly, the one who comes "boldly before the throne of grace"[47] must not come as the pompous and prideful Pharisee[48] but as the submissive and supplicating Savior "with strong crying and tears."[49]

When the freed slave, Sojourner Truth, related the pathetic story of her child who had been stolen from her and sold, she said: "I don't rightly know which way to turn; but I went to the Lord and I said to him, 'O Lord, if I was as rich as you be, and you was as poor as I be, I'd help you, you know I would; and oh, do help me!' and I felt sure he would, and he did."

Becoming Specific With God

"How do I love thee? Let me count the ways," suggests a desire to know the one loved intimately and specifically. Similarly, the pray-er who lays hold on God's willingness gets to know Him intimately who prays without ceasing in a specific way.

To avoid vain repetition, one must learn to make specific transactions with the Lord God. A written contract, for example, is quite specific Or it *cannot* be enforced. So, too, when one taps into prayer power, one should come to regard the petition as a "contract" with God.

When blind Bartimaeus cried, "Jesus, thou Son of David, have mercy on me," his stated request was quite general. Accordingly, when Jesus asked, "What wilt thou?" He charged the man to be specific. Surely, He must have known what the blind beggar wanted with all of his heart, mind, and soul. Yet, the omniscient Savior required a specific request. Hence, Bartimaeus cried, "Lord, that I may receive my sight." Whereupon, he "immediately received his sight."[50]

Hannah was also specific with God. In the bitterness of her soul, she wept sore because she "had no children." Her agonizing with God was so great that when she came before the temple, the priest Eli thought she was drunk and was thereby profaning the temple. Though she spoke *only* in her heart, Samuel tells us what she must have constantly reminded him: "You are God's answer to my prayer."[51] For Hannah vowed, "Oh Lord of hosts, if thou wilt indeed look on the affliction of thine handmaiden, and remember me, and not forget thine handmaiden, but wilt give unto thine handmaiden a man child, then I will give him unto the Lord all the days of his life."[52] Notice that Hannah even asked for a "man child," and the Lord God knowing the absolutely unselfish nature of the petition, granted the request exactly as presented.

The usual representation of Elijah is as a great prophet and prayer warrior. Yet, James presents him as a "man subject to like passions as we are."[53] Thus, Elijah was just an ordinary person -- like you and me. Yet, he knew how to prevail in prayer because he knew how to agonize specifically. James tells us that Elijah "prayed earnestly that it might not rain, and it rained not on the earth by the space of three years and six months. And he prayed again, and the heaven gave rain, and the earth brought forth her fruit."[54]

Petitions that produce powerful results are fervent and specific. Moreover, every A C T of prayer should become definite and distinct. In **Adoration,** David cried, "Seven times a day do I praise thee because of the righteous

judgments."[55] In **Confession**, it is not enough to admit
that we are sinners. We must confess our sins --
specifically and penitently -- so that the Lord God can be
"faithful and just to forgive us our sins."[56]   In
Thanksgiving, the Thessalonian Christians learned, "In
every thing give thanks, for this is the will of God in
Christ Jesus concerning you."[57]   Notice that the word
every thing is not compound, but separated, suggesting a
sensitivity of the pray-er to be thankful for each and
every single thing, as it occurs. As if in summary, to the
Philippians Paul prayerfully praised the Lord, and
having reminded them of the need for repentance for a
specific strife, advised them:

> *"Be careful for nothing; but in every thing (i.e.,
> each thing) by prayer and supplication with
> thanksgiving let your requests be made known
> unto God. And the peace of God, which passes
> all understanding, shall keep your hearts and
> minds through Christ Jesus."*[58]

Careful consideration of the major functions of prayer
power   --   **ADORATION,   CONFESSION,
THANKSGIVING, SUPPLICATION** -- leads to the
inescapable conclusion that all of these "labors"[59] are for
the most part specific and definite. Not all Biblical
expressions are specific. Is not the very essence of
becoming "instant in prayer"[60] a suggestion of
definiteness?

Keep The House Clean

Every person who cleans a house knows that he/she
must watch carefully to keep it clean. Jesus pictured for
us a once-demon-possessed man whose spiritual house

had been made clean, "swept and garnished." Yet, because of a lack of vigilance, seven other spirits later came into the house making the last state of the man worse than the first.[61] As the apostle Peter pictured it, "The dog is turned to his own vomit again; and the sow that was washed to her wallowing in the mire."[62]

Jesus found it necessary to cleanse the temple in Jerusalem not once but twice: at the beginning and at the very end of His earthly ministry. Because of this, the "keeper" of the temple hated Him greatly. And so, after the second cleansing, He left the city He loved and had tried so often to gather its children together, "... even as a hen gathered her chickens under her wings. Ye would not! Behold your house is left unto you desolate."[63]

But why, Lord Jesus?

To the scribes and Pharisees, Jesus reserved the stinging rebuke, "Hypocrites: for ye devour widows' houses and for a pretense make long prayers."[64]

To his disciples, Jesus enjoined, "Watch and pray lest ye enter into temptation."[65] Then having found His closest companions asleep during their prayer watch -- remember that it was after midnight when He confronted them -- He challenged, "Why sleep ye? Rise and pray."[66]

STOP

Child of the King, determine to set aside Specific Times Of Prayer, thereby keeping your spiritual temple cleansed that you may engage in true worship. For "the eyes of the Lord are over the righteous, and His ears are open unto their prayers."[67] Therefore, set aside Specific Times Of Prayer to "rise and pray."[68]

In a village, natives converted to Christ made it their habit to go into the bush to pray, by paths that their pious feet had beaten out. At such times, as their prayer would become irregular, or cease altogether, the grass would grow on their path to prayer. Is it so that the lush grass of negligence has grown up as a jungle about our souls? Has its canopy obscured the face of God in Christ? May it not be so!

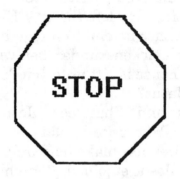

Chapter IV

PRAYER POWER TO CHANGE GOD'S MIND

> "God repented of the evil He said He would do
> unto them; and He did it not."
> -Jonah 3:10

"HE CHANGES NOT"

"Nothing is permanent but change" may well refer to everything but to the Lord God. For he is eternal; from age to age, the same. As God told Malachi, **"I AM THE LORD. I CHANGE NOT."**[1] Hence, people praise Him even to this day for His "unchanging hand." Thus, those who seek to know Him as the eternal and unchanging Lord God must also conform to His unchanging will.

WHY PRAY?

The carping critic perceives a paradox: an unchanging God with and unchanging will who makes changes at the request of mere man. So convincing is his challenge that he buries his talent; for there is, indeed, not always a clear connection between investment and return.[2]

It is a tragedy indeed that so many refuse to believe in God because they see no clear connection between prayer and providence. Yet, the greater tragedy is that so many saints have failed to pray. According to a national survey reported by a church of Christ in Denver, Colorado, fully 25 percent of the born-again beautiful[3] admit that they have no personal prayer life. Many others -- who do pray -- cannot claim much progress in their Christian lives.

These pray-ers, moreover, maintain nagging doubts as to whether the Lord God really answers prayer.

Despite the detractions of so many, there is a plethora of evidence that of all the "exceeding great and precious promises"[4] given to "them that have obtained like precious faith with us through the righteousness of God and our Savior Jesus Christ,"[5] none is more certain than the one that GOD ANSWERS PRAYER. "Call upon me and I will answer thee."[6] "Ask and it shall be given unto you."[7] These divine injunctions encourage the faithful to pray. Exclusive of the Psalms, which form a prayer-book of their own, the Bible records no fewer that 650 definite prayers, of which no fewer than 450 have recorded answers. Nearly all of these answers are in the affirmative, for God's favorite answer is "Yes."

HOW IS IT POSSIBLE?

The Bible is replete with references where the Lord God has changed His mind. In *every* case, prayer was the *exclusive* means for man to prevail.

PRAYER POWER TO SPARE CITIES

When the Lord revealed to Abraham that the sin of Sodom and Gomorrah is "very grievous,"[8] Abraham pleaded with the Lord not to destroy the righteous with the wicked. Thus, he prayed that if fifty righteous souls were still in these cities, the Lord would "spare all the places for their sakes."[9] Again and again, Abraham, who described himself as "but dust and ashes"[10] reduced the number of the righteous -- to 45, to 40, to 30, to 20, and finally to 10. Five times Abraham changed God's mind! When Abraham had so persuaded the Lord, the angels who examined the city according to the Lord's instructions[11] found only Lot and his family who were righteous.   Fewer than ten souls!   Even so, was it not because of prayer power that the Lord spared the righteous ones?

Jonah preached to Ninevah," an exceeding great city of three days' journey"[12] whose wickedness was so repulsive that the Lord had determined to destroy the city 40 days after Jonah's first cry against the city.[13]   Yet, when the people believed God, they fasted and "cried mightily unto God: yea, let them turn every one from his evil way, and from the violence that is in their hands.[14]   Because of their penitent prayer, "God repented of the evil that He had said that He would do unto them; and He did it not.[15]

The Lord God spared perhaps as many as 600,000 people from destruction *solely* because of prayer power. Spared for nearly 200 years, the evil of Ninevah so infuriated the Lord that he finally destroyed it.[16]   Would not the Lord have changed his mind a second time if the people had repented and prayed as they did the first time?

PRAYER POWER TO PRESERVE NATIONS

The Israelites had experienced 430 years of slavery in Egypt.   At long last, when the bondage became unbearable, their "cry came up unto God."[17]   Accordingly, because of their re-discovery *as a people* of prayer power, their slave masters actually drove them out of the land of bondage and finally set them free.   Would not their bondage have continued had they not prayed for deliverance?

Yet, when Moses, their God-chosen leader, was on Mt. Sinai receiving the Covenant, the people turned in their hearts back to bondage.   So as to be well-received upon their return to Egypt, they melted down their jewelry and built a golden calf.

The Lord became so angry that He told Moses, "Let me alone, that my wrath may wax hot against them: and I will make of thee a great nation."[18]

Moses prayed to the Lord to "turn from thy fierce wrath, and repent of this evil against thy people." Hence, the Lord changed His mind and did not destroy the people as He wanted to do.[19] What amazing prayer power to spare the lives of over two million people!

> *"He said He would destroy them, had not Moses stood before Him in the breach."*[20]

PRAYER POWER TO EXTEND LIFE

During a severe illness, King Hezekiah received a message from the Lord God by the prophet Isaiah, "Set thine house in order; for thou shalt die, and not live."[21] Yet, as Hezekiah lay upon his bed, he agonized ("wept sore") in prayer, begging the Lord to recall "how I have walked before thee in truth and with a perfect heart, and have done what is good in thy sight."[22]

The Lord God heard in heaven and answered within minutes:

> *"And it came to pass, afore Isaiah was gone out of the middle court, that the word of the Lord came to him, saying 'Turn again, and tell Hezekiah, the captain of my people, "Thus saith the Lord, the God of David thy father, I have heard thy prayer, I have seen thy tears: behold I will heal thee: on the third day thou shalt go up to the house of the Lord. And I will add unto thy days fifteen years; and I will deliver out of the hand of the king of Assyria; and I will defend this city for mine own sake, and for my servant David's sake."*[23]

Let us take not that the Lord God answered the petition exactly as presented. Even so, the man of God also used human methods of healing. For Isaiah stated, "Take a lump of figs and lay it over the boil."[24]

Is not the example of Hezekiah the spirit of the instruction of James to the saint who becomes sick:

> *"Let him call for the elders of the church; and let them pray over him, anointing him with oil in the name of the Lord. And the prayer of faith shall save the sick, and the Lord shall raise him up; and if he have committed sins, they shall be forgiven him."*[25]

PRAYER POWER TO CHANGE THE WEATHER

"Everybody talks about the weather, but nobody does anything about it." Yet, this "delicious" proverb has become a "fact" for even the "faithful" ones. After all, doesn't the rain fall upon the evil as well as upon the good?[26] Yet, the Bible reveals that prayer power has been sufficient to change God's mind about the weather -- with significant results.

Job revealed that God had weighed the waters by measure and had made a decree for the rain.[27]

The Bible reveals that there are weather patterns that have borne direct correlation with the Lord God's response to the evil and the good of mankind. Because "the wickedness of men was great in the earth, and every imagination of the thoughts of his heart was only evil continually ...and the earth was filled with violence,"[28] the Lord God completely disrupted the weather patterns and sent a flood to destroy all of the evil persons in the world.[29] He saved only eight righteous souls from the flood.[30]

Besides saving the righteous from the world-wide flood, the Lord God revealed to his chosen people, the Israelites, that the rain would not vary from its due season, that it would be sufficient for the land to yield her increase and for trees to yield her fruit.[31]   Even so, the Lord God required that the people walk in His statutes, and keep His commandments.[32]

When Elijah prayed that there would be no dew or rain,[33] the king "did evil in the sight of the Lord above all that were before him."[34] He led the people into great evil. Accordingly, one may conclude that this was in keeping with the Lord God's decree.   Yet, consider that when Elijah prayed again three and one-half years later for the drought to end, the evil was perhaps even worse than before. For Elijah had to flee for his own life. Believing himself to be the only faithful person left in the land, he even prayed for God to take away his life.[35]

The Lord God had promised that "if I shut up the heaven that there be no rain,"[36] penitent prayer power would cause Him to "heal the land."[37]   Indeed, He required prayer of the people as the necessary and sufficient conditions to end the drought. Yet, when Elijah prayed for rain, the people still had not turned from their evil ways. Only 7,000 throughout the land had not bowed to Baal. Even so, the Lord God sent a "great rain."[38] Was it not prayer power that changed God's mind about the weather?

CONCLUSION

When Jesus began to teach his disciples to pray, He made it plain that it wasn't just the words but the urgency of the request that would prevail. He told of a person who went to a friend at midnight to ask for some bread to share with another friend. Jesus pointed out that the man aroused from sleep would not arise even for his friend. It was the importunity that changed his mind.[39] On another occasion, as Jesus warned that men ought always to pray and not to faint, He told of an unjust judge who neither feared God nor regarded man. Yet, a widow who came with fire in her eyes demanding vengeance from her adversary caused the judge to be "troubled" and to grant her request "lest by her continual coming she weary me."[40] Then after the Lord said, "Hear what the unjust says," he asked:

> *"Shall not God avenge His own elect, which cry day and night unto Him, though He bear long with them? I tell you that He will avenge then speedily. Nevertheless when the Son of Man cometh, shall he find faith on the earth?"*[41]

Jesus had seen the pretenders of His day. He warned of self-righteous pray-ers who sought to justify themselves.[42] He revealed that repentance was necessary for all. For example, He referred to the collapse of a tower in Siloam where eighteen persons fell to their deaths and to the Galilean whose blood Pilate had mingled with heathen sacrifices. He asked if the present company saw the victims as sinners above all others. He then concluded in each case, "No!" "Except ye repent, ye shall all likewise perish."[43]

If prayer power is sufficient to change the Lord God's mind, why don't saints really pray for the "good gifts" of the Father who is far wiser and far more capable of answering those who call upon Him?[44] What limit is there but lack of faith in prayer power?

Chapter V

PRAYER POWER THROUGH THE AGES

"The desire of all nations shall come."
-Haggai 2:7

The Proper Focus

Jesus is the "desire of all nations."[1] Truly, all history revolves around the "Word that was made flesh and dwelt among us."[2] Our very calendars remind us that time is either "Before Christ" (B.C.) or "Anno Domini" (A.D.). Thus, although the Biblical history of mankind shows three distinct dispensations in which the Lord God has allowed men to approach Him, prayer power relationships reveal Jesus Christ as "the mystery...hidden from ages and from generations."[3] The proper focus of the Patriarchal Period, the Mosical Dispensation, as well as the Christian Age is Jesus as the Christ.

The Patriarchal Period

When the Lord God spoke all of creation into existence, He said, "Let us make man."[4] In so stating, He affirmed that the Word that was with God was God.[5] He also echoed the consequent oneness when He prayed to the Father that "...they (the disciples) might be one, even as we are."[6]

Having created man "in our image, after our likeness,"[7] the Lord God expected man to communicate with His creator (Elohim) and covenant maker (Yahweh) in an obedient manner. The primary method of sustaining the proper relationship is prayer, for the Lord God created man as a praying person.

For simplification, let us consider prayer as the realization of need and the finding of opportunity for talking with the Lord God. From the beginning of the course of man, prayer then is a conversation fixed in heaven.[8]

The first mention of man "calling upon the name of the Lord"[9] occurs with the birth of Enos, the 235th year from the beginning. This is "social worship."[10] For the passage uses the plural: "men." Even so, no matter how distressing the dialogue between God and Adam, the first father, evidently man had from the very first learned to talk with God according to His covenant.[11] Does not John Milton, the blind poet, accurately portray the prayerful state of the first patriarch when he introduced Adam as advising Eve-

> *"What better can we do, than to the place*
> *Repairing, where he judged us, prostrate fall*
> *Before Him reverent; and there confess*
> *Humbly our faults, and pardon beg; with tears*
> *Watering the ground, and with our sighs the air*
> *Frequenting?"*

When the first patriarch discontinued prayerful obedience, the Lord God cast him and his wife out of paradise and away from the tree of life.[12] With the punishment of man came the Lord's promise addressed to Satan, "I will put enmity between thee and the woman, and between thy seed and her seed; it shall bruise thy head and thou shalt bruise his heel."[13] Thus, the Lord God prophesied of Jesus. For only the man has seed; yet He spoke of "her seed," and in so doing foretold that Jesus, though Himself bruised, would deliver a crushing blow to Satan. Do we not find fulfillment of this in the death, burial and resurrection of Jesus? Was not this the Son of God "manifested that He might destroy the works of the devil?"[14]

After Adam's sin, and despite the faithfulness of a lineage of patriarchs, the earth became full of wickedness of every imagination so that God used a flood to destroy all of mankind except for eight souls, Noah and his family.[15]

After the flood, Noah's first thought was to build an altar.[16] This special construction became a place of sacrifice and prayer. The next great patriarch, Abraham, also built an altar and there "called upon the name of the Lord."[17] The altar, thus identified through Abraham, became the slaughter place of Jesus.[18]

Abraham became the first "friend of God."[19] Accordingly, he knew the limitless nature of prayer power is evident in his intercession for sin-filled Sodom and Gomorrah.[20] Abraham could bargain with God on behalf of the righteous. In response to his prayer,[21] God could commit the greatest promise of the ages:

> *"I will make of thee a great nation...and in thee shall all families of the earth be blessed."*[22]

The first part of the promise came true with the birth of the Israelite nation; the second, with the birth of Jesus Christ.[23] "For by one Spirit are we all baptized into one body, whether we be Jews or Gentiles, whether we be bond or free."[24]

The birth of Isaac to a couple so far beyond the time of childbearing proved that through prayer nothing is impossible with God.[25] Moreover, reckoning that God could raise Isaac from the grave to fulfill His promise,[26] Abraham obeyed God's command to sacrifice Isaac upon the altar. Even so, were there not sobs of prayer throughout the three-day trip to the top of Mount Moriah? What earthly father would not have begged without ceasing that "thine only son, whom thou lovest"[27] be spared?

Could we not say that Isaac's blood was not shed? After all, God provided a lamb as the sacrifice instead of Isaac. Yet, clearly, Isaac's blood was shed -- as it were -- at calvary by Jesus Christ, a direct descendant of Abraham and Isaac. Jesus said, "Abraham rejoiced to see my day; and he saw it, and was glad."[28] Did he not see Jesus when he looked prayerfully through his tear-filled eyes and saw the lamb caught in the thicket by his horns?[29] Was not this "the lamb of God that taketh away the sin of the world?"[30] Was not this lamb, in a figure, Jesus the Christ revealed in a moment of Abraham's fervent, effectual prayer?

The Mosaical Dispensation

The praying patriarch Abraham became the friend of God. So, too, did the great lawgiver Moses; for "the Lord spoke unto Moses face to face as a man speaketh unto his friend."[31] Indeed, Moses was also a man of prayer whose prevailing power with God was virtually unlimited and foreshadowed Jesus as the Christ. For the Lord told Moses:

> *"The Lord thy God will raise...them up a prophet from among their brethren, like unto thee, and will put my words in his mouth; and he shall speak unto them all that I shall command him. And it shall come to pass, that whosoever will not hearken unto my words which he shall speak in my name, I will require it of him."*[32]

The prophet who would tell all things was Jesus.[33] For by His own testimony in prayer to the Father, He said, "I have given unto them the words which thou gavest me."[34]

Even as Moses first came to hearken to the voice of God, his prayer was to know who God really was. God's answer pointed not only to Himself but to Jesus as well: "**I AM THAT I AM**."[35] For Jesus was referred to as "the Alpha and Omega (the beginning and the end.")[36] Thus, he could say, "Before Abraham was, I am,"[37] for Jesus Christ is the same yesterday, and today and forever."[38] Evidently, by meeting God, Moses in prayerful dialogue was also meeting Him who was "one with God," Jesus Christ - **THE GREAT I AM**, before whom "every knee shall bow and every tongue shall confess."[39]

In response to Moses' petition for signs that God would help him, God gave him a rod. Not only did Moses use this sign of prayer power to part the Red Sea[40] and to enable the Israelites to defeat the Amalekites,[41] he also pointed to Jesus when he used the rod to smite the rock[42] from which water "flowed like a river."[43] For as Paul instructed the Corinthian Christians, "They drank of that Spiritual rock that followed them: and that rock was Christ."[44]

Perhaps, one may realize the significance of God's anger with Moses for striking the rock the second time by remembering that the "striking" of Jesus so that His water and His blood flowed forth was to be done only once. or Jesus died once for all.[45] As punishment for striking the rock, Moses could not, during his lifetime, cross over Jordan into the promised land. Even so, some authorities place the Mount of Transfiguration within the land of Canaan. Thus, after His death, He may well have received God's gracious answer to be in the promised land with the greatest pray-er of all time - Jesus Christ.

Moses offered himself as a sacrifice for his people. For upon discovery of the golden calf as a monument of madness, Moses prayed, "Oh, this people have sinned a great sin, and have made the gods of gold. Yet, now, if thou wilt forgive their sin - ; and if not, blot me, I pray thee, out of thy book which thou hast written."[46] But God rejected his offer in prayer, choosing instead His only begotten Son to die for the sins of man."[47]

When Moses ascended Mount Sinai to receive God's commands, he spent each of the two forty-day periods in prayer.[48] Then when he came down from the Mount, his face shone.[49] His intimate prayerful communication with God foreshadowed the prayer power of Jesus whose entire body and even His clothes shone "as He prayed on the Mount of Transfiguration."[50]

Even at the end of his life, Moses' first concern was for his people. And so he prayed for a new leader, "a man over the congregation, which may go out before them, and which may go in before them, and which may lead them out, and which may bring them in; that the congregation of the Lord be not as sheep which have no shepherd."[51] How very near to the prayer-heart of Jesus who promised His apostles "another comforter," the Holy Spirit of truth[52] for His church[53] where there would be leaders after the apostles - elders, deacons, evangelists, and teachers guided by His inspired work once delivered for all.[54]

Of all the Mosical Dispensation prophets until Christ "there arose not a prophet...like unto Moses, whom the Lord knew face to face."[55] Yet, there were other great men and women who fixed their correspondence in heaven, whose prevailing prayers pointed to Christ.

Joshua's prayer for victory produced a miracle, for "the sun stood still in the midst of heaven, and hasted not to go down about a whole day."[56] How very much like the day Christ died when His loving prayers brought a three-hour-long darkness at noon, earthquakes, and resurrections from the dead.[57] Oh, what power there was in the prayers of Joshua and of Jesus, both of whom were saviors of their people.

The scriptures tell that time and again the people would fall into captivity because of their great sin. In all, the Israelites spent nearly 100 years of bondage in the land of Canaan because of their sin. Each time they prayed for a deliverer, the Lord gave them what they asked for - judges: Othniel,[58] Ehud,[59] Deborah and Barak,[60] Gideon,[61] Jephthah....[62] So, too, as the Israelites prayed for a deliverer from the bondage of sin,[63] the Lord God sent his only Son as the redeemer not only for the Israelites but for all peoples of the earth.[64]

Scripture does not declare that all of the judges were God's answers to prayer. Yet, may not one reasonably infer this? In one case, however, only one of the people prayed for Samuel to become a judge, namely, Hannah, the mother-to-be. Because Hannah was barren, she was in bitterness of soul, and prayed unto the Lord, and wept sore.[65] So distraught was she that when she prayed before the temple, Eli, the priest, accused her of being drunk and thereby profaning the temple. Yet, Hannah persisted, and her prayer was to change the course of history. "She vowed a vow and said:

> *"O Lord of hosts, if thou wilt indeed look on the affliction of thine handmaiden, and remember me and not forget thine handmaid, but will give unto thine handmaid a man child, then I will give him unto the Lord all the days of his life."*[66]

Notice how fervently Hannah begged God without ceasing until Eli answered and said, "Go in peace: and the God of Israel grant thee thy petition that thou hast asked of Him."[67] And so, because the Lord answered her petition - even to the pre-determining of the sex of the child,

Hannah in her prayer of thanksgiving prophesied of the coming of Christ:

> *"The adversaries of the Lord shall be broken to pieces; out of heaven shall he thunder upon them: the Lord shall judge the ends of the earth; and he shall give strength unto his king, and exalt the horn of his anointed."*[68]

Samuel was the last of the fourteen judges of Israel. When he was old, the people asked for a king. And so, Samuel whose very name means "asked of God," felt rejected and so stated to the Lord in prayer. Yet, the Lord said, "They have not rejected thee, but they have rejected me, that I should not reign over them.[69] So, too, the people rejected Jesus as the "king of the Jews"[70] that he not reign over them. And in rejecting the Son of God, they rejected the Father as well.[71]

During the days when the judges ruled, one encounters the prayers of other faithful women. Upon the birth of a child to Ruth and Boaz, there were women who cried, "Blessed be the Lord."[72] Yet, the praise was not to the actual parents but to Naomi, the mother of Ruth by marriage. For because of the untimely death of Naomi's sons and of her husband, she said, "Call me Mara," a name meaning "bitter."[73] But upon the birth of a child to her daughter-in-law, Ruth, now married to Boaz, Naomi's kinsman, her countenance became "pleasant," the very meaning of her name, Naomi. Accordingly, she made her blessing to the Lord; and the Lord turned the prayer into prophecy, for the child was named Obed, the father of Jesse, the father of David.[74] All of these names appear in the genealogy of Jesus Christ.[75]

Even though the people had rejected the leadership of Samuel and had demanded a king instead, Samuel, the last of the judges, continued to pray for the people.

Indeed, he said that he would be sinning if he should cease to pray for them.[76] Yet, even as Samuel prophesied of the harsh rule a king would bring, he prayerfully anointed Saul as the first king.[77]

Saul was initially a prayerful king who sought counsel of God.[78] All too quickly, however, he neglected prayer power to the point of rebellion against God. As a consequence, David, who came "in the name of the Lord of hosts," received the kingdom.[79] Whereupon, this shepherd-king, a man after God's own heart, wrote many prayer-songs that comprise the book of Psalms, which are chocked full of prophecies of the shepherd-king Jesus. Consider the following, for example:

> *"I will declare the decree: the Lord hath said unto me, "Thou art my son; this day have I begotten thee."*[80]

> *"FOR GOD SO LOVED THE WORLD THAT HE GAVE HIS ONLY BEGOTTEN SON, THAT WHOSOEVER BELIEVETH IN HIM SHOULD NOT PERISH, BUT HAVE EVERLASTING LIFE.'*[81]

O O O O O

O O O O O

> *"Thou wilt not leave my soul in hell; neither wilt thou suffer thine Holy one to see corruption."*[82]

> *"HE WHOM GOD RAISED AGAIN, SAW NO CORRUPTION.'*[83]

O O O O O

O   O   O   O   O

"My God, my God why hast thou forsaken Me?
Why art thou so far from helping Me, and from
the words of my roaring."   "They part my
garments among them, and cast lots upon my
vesture."[84]

"JESUS CRIED WITH A LOUD VOICE, 'MY
GOD, MY GOD, WHY HAST THOU
FORSAKEN ME?"[85]

"THEY CRUCIFIED HIM AND PARTED HIS
GARMENTS, CASTING LOTS."[86]

O   O   O   O   O

O   O   O   O   O

"Into thine hand I commit my spirit: thou has
redeemed me, O Lord God of Truth."[87]

"JESUS CRIED, 'FATHER, INTO THY
HANDS I COMMEND MY SPIRIT."[88]

O   O   O   O   O

O   O   O   O   O

Thus, the Psalmist David praised God in prayer so
powerfully that much of it became prophecy of the
greatest pray-er of all ages, the Lord Jesus Christ.

When David died, he was still in prayer. And so, his
son, Solomon, began his reign in prayer for wisdom.[89] It
is little wonder that as God granted his request. Solomon

spoke 3,000 proverbs and wrote 1,005 songs, one of which is by symbol almost entirely a prophecy of Jesus.[90] Moreover, Solomon built the great temple in Jerusalem as a place for every man's prayer and supplication.[91] Nonetheless, the temple did not so remain. For by the time of Jesus' ministry, it had become a house of merchandise.[92] Consequently, Jesus drove out all the profiteers, declaring that not only the physical temple but the spiritual dwelling place of God, the faithful obedient person himself, must become a "house of prayer."[93]

During the subsequent succession of kings, prophets of God performed miracles through prayer power. For example, Elijah prayed for a drought that lasted for three-and-a-half years.[94] He prayed again and the heavens gave rain.[95] Elijah and Elisha each prayed successfully for the resurrection of a dead child.[96]

Once again these prevailers in prayer pointed to the prince of pray-ers, Jesus Christ. For He would demonstrate not only His control of nature by changing water into wine[97] and by walking on the stormy sea that caused even those in a ship to fear for their lives,[98] but He would also demonstrate His power over life and death by raising Lazarus from the grave[99] and even Himself, the singularly greatest miracle and most significant event in all of history.[100]

Despite the precious prayers of the prophets, most of the kings were so evil that they ignored the prayer-invoked prophecies that forecast calamity. And so, there came according to the prophecy of Daniel a succession of conquests by foreign powers: first, the Babylonians (606 B.C.); second, the Medo-Persian (538 B.C.); third, the Greeks (331 B.C.); and the fourth, the Romans (65 B.C.). In response to Daniel's prayer for power to interpret King Nebuchadnezzar's dream, God again used prayer to reveal that in the days of the Roman kings the God of heaven would use a stone not made with hands to break into pieces "all these kingdoms" and in so doing "set up a kingdom that shall never be destroyed."[101] That stone of truth was Christ and the kingdom is His church.[102]

The Christian Age

As a consequence of their prayers, both patriarch and prophet saw the coming of the Messiah. And, at last, there came a voice "crying in the wilderness, 'Make straight the way of the Lord.'"[103] "Thus, John the Baptist preached, "Repent ye: for the kingdom of heaven is at hand,"[104] And indeed, the prayer power of Jesus demonstrated that He was both Lord and Christ.[105]

The promise of Christ that he would build His church[106] was realized on the first Day of Pentecost after His resurrection. And the church was ushered in with prayer and supplication that had continued without ceasing after the ascension of Jesus.[107]

At the conclusion of the first gospel sermon, the apostle Peter showed how every sinner - and that's every person who ever lived[108] - could obtain covenanted prayer power in the kingdom of Christ:

> *"Repent and be baptized every one of you for the remission of sins, and ye shall receive the gift of the Holy Ghost."*[109]

As each believing person penitently confessed his faith in the risen Lord and had his sins washed away in the watery grave of baptism,[110] the Lord added that person to the church,[111] the congregation(s) of believers - both in private and in public assembly - continued their fellowship in prayer according to the apostles' doctrine.[112]

From the very first, these converts to Christ participated in:

> *"The fellowship of the mystery, which from the beginning of the world hath been hid in God, who created all things by Christ: to the intent that now unto the principalities and powers in heavenly places might be known by the church, the manifold wisdom of God."*[113]

And, as the apostle Paul wrote from prison shortly before his execution, the most significant consequence of being in the church was the access to the Father through our Lord Jesus Christ in prayer.[114]

The church did not come into existence without severe persecution. Yet, the church prevailed and indeed multiplied because "they lifted up their voice to God with one accord."[115]

When, for example, Peter and John had healed a man lame from his mother's womb, the religious leaders arrested these apostles. The prayer meeting that followed actually shook the rafters and enabled the apostles to preach with great boldness and power.[116] Not long afterwards, "when Herod killed James, the brother of John with the sword" and then kept Peter in prison, "prayer was made without ceasing of the church,"[117] Peter was released in a manner beyond their ability to ask or think.[118]

At other times, when the lives of saints were endangered, they prayed and praised the Lord. Paul and Silas thereby effected a miraculous release from a prison cell.[119] Even so, perhaps the greatest prayer power that brought freedom forever was that of Stephen who, when he was being stoned for preaching Jesus, prayed, "Lord, lay not this sin to their charge."[120] Was it not his intercession for his murderers that caused the heaven to open and for him to see the greatest intercessor of all time, Jesus "standing on the right hand of God"?[121]

The Lord allowed Stephen to be martyred for His cause. Yet, though Paul prayed that his own soul be lost so that his brethren and kinsmen would be saved, God did not allow Paul to be so sacrificed.[122]   And despite the testimony that preaching of the crucified Christ would be a stumbling block to the Jews,[123] God is not willing that any should perish but that all should come to repentance.[124]

Besides external persecution, the early church faced internal strife. And here again, the answer to the problem was prayer power. When, for example, the Grecian widows were being "neglected in the daily ministration," seven men were selected to handle the matter so that the apostles could give themselves continually to prayer and to the ministry of the word.[125]

There were those outside the church who remained ignorant of salvation through faith in Christ. Yet, they prayed, and their utterances went up, as with Cornelius, as "a memorial before God."[126]   Then, when Saul of Tarsus, the greatest persecutor of all, learned humility through a vision that left him blind, he was in prayer for three days.[127] After his baptism, he went to the temple to pray -- but now with a covenanted relationship made possible by the blood shed by Jesus Christ,[128] the prince of pray-ers and the most powerful advocate ever known;[129] for "He is able to save them to the uttermost who come unto God by Him."[130]

The first-century church undertook special missions and ministries *only* by prayer and fasting. When, for example, Paul and Barnabas began their missionary journey, they "fasted and prayed."[131]   Again, with the ordination of elders in every church, it was in each case by prayer with fasting.[132] Moreover, when Paul called the elders of Ephesus to Miletus to warn them of grievous wolves who would not spare the flock, "He kneeled down and prayed with them all. And they all wept sore."[133]

Re-Focus

The true history of mankind, as revealed by prayer power, ever points to Jesus Christ as the central figure of all ages.

A young man was just starting out upon his work as a minister in London, England. He asked an aged minister who had spent a lifetime of service for some advice. The old minister replied:

> "You know that in every village or hamlet, though it be hidden in the folds of the mountain or wrapped around by the far-off sea, in every clump of farmhouses, you can find a road which, if you follow it, will take you to London."

> "Just so, every text you choose to preach from in the Bible will have a road that leads to Christ. Be sure you find that road, and follow it, be careful not to miss it once."

The old minister spoke the truth affirmed in this chapter: All of the precious paths throughout history point to the Lord Jesus Christ -- in his blessed holy name, Amen!

Chapter VI

THE PRAYER POWER OF JESUS

> "Lord, teach us to pray."
> -Luke 11:1

My Way

The strains of the once popular song, "I did it my way," have lingered as a contrasting theme to the Biblical reminder, "God's ways are not man's ways."[1] "For the wisdom of this world is foolishness with God."[2]

The fact that God does not usually do things according to the dictates of "logic" frequently invites the ridicule of skeptics.

♦ Would the wisdom of man have captured the city of Jericho by having the people walk around it blowing horns?

♦ What logician would have advised Gideon to stock up on water jars before his battle with the Midianites?

♦ What counselor to a would-be king would suggest riding into the camp of the enemy on a donkey?

♦ What person in his right mind would ask another to die, be resurrected, then leave the scene of victory?

Truly, God's wisdom is not human but divine.

The essential problem facing the Christian today is the insistence upon doing things his own way and not God's way. Thus, every word, and every action must become the Lord's way rather than "my way." Accordingly, the methodology for knowing Him as Yahweh (covenant maker) -- and Elohim (creator) -- Lord God - is to learn the true power of prayer from Him who was one with God and "glorified not himself to be made an high priest."[3] Rather, He offered up prayers and supplications with strong crying and tears...and was heard in that He feared."[4] Even in the moments when terror filled His soul and tears came as drops of blood, Jesus prayed, "Not my will but thine be done."[5]

Preparation By Prayer

Turn the pages of the gospel of Matthew, Mark, Luke, John, and you will find that almost every opening shows someone in prayer.

Even before the birth of the Messiah, faithful hearts prayerfully yearned for the coming of the Messiah. Luke relates that when Zacharias, the priest, was executing office before God...burning incense....the whole multitude of the people were praying.[6] Then Zacharias saw an angel at the altar who told him not to fear, "for thy prayer is heard."[7] Oh, the great joy that Zacharias must have known in the consequent promise, "Thy wife Elizabeth shall bear thee a son, and thou shalt call his name John."[8] Thus, when John became the Baptist and announced Jesus as "the lamb of God that takes away the sins of the world,"[9] was it not further response to the prayer of Zacharias?

Luke also shows that prayers attended the birth of Jesus. For as the "angel of the Lord" announced the "good tidings of great joy,"[10] "suddenly there was with the angel a multitude of the heavenly host praising God and saying, 'Glory to God in the highest, and on earth, peace, good will to men.'"[11]

Shortly after the birth of Jesus, Simon, a devout man who had been told by the Holy Ghost that he would not die until he had seen the Savior, took the infant Jesus in his arms and prayed,

> *"Lord, now lettest thou thy servant depart in peace, according to thy word; for mine eyes have seen thy salvation, which thou has prepared before the face of all people; a light to lighten the Gentiles and the glory of thy people Israel."*[12]

At the same time there entered one Anna, a prophetess who "served God with fasting and prayers night and day," and "gave thanks unto the Lord and spoke of Jesus to all them that looked for redemption in Jerusalem."[13]

Surely, as those at the time of His birth persevered in prayer, Jesus Himself also becomes one who filled His life with prayer. Although the first recorded prayer of Jesus occurred when He was about thirty years of age, He must have engaged unceasingly in prayer as he "increased in wisdom and stature and in favor with God and man."[14] For His family was devoutly faithful. His Uncle Zacharias was a priest whose prayer the Lord God heard,[15] and His mother Mary was most holy among women. Moreover, faithful Jews continued a prayerful watch for the oft-promised and long-awaited Messiah.

A Ministry Of Prayer

Jesus practiced what he preached, for His prayer life was His way of life. Indeed, Jesus showed how prayer *is* life, for without prayer there is spiritual death. Prayer power was never more of a living reality than when Jesus prayed.

He Began In Prayer

At the very onset of His ministry, Jesus demonstrated prayer power. Luke tells us that as Jesus was being baptized, He was "praying."[16] The present participle suggests an on-going correspondence between being baptized and praying. Thus, as He was going down into the water, was being immersed, and was being raised he was praying. And the result of that prayerful submission was that

> *"The heaven was opened, and the Holy Spirit descended in a bodily shape like a dove upon Him, and a voice from heaven, which said, Thou art my beloved Son; in thee I am well pleased."'*[17]

He Continued in Prayer

Throughout His ministry, Jesus was continually in prayer. Subsequent to His baptism, and during the first two years, the gospel accounts reveal three times that Jesus prayed.

During His first preaching tour, Mark relates:

> *"In the morning, rising up a great while before day, He went out, and departed into a solitary place and there prayed."*[22]

Although the preceding day had been extremely exhausting, we still see Jesus engaged in prayer. Was it to overcome the lure of popularity or to renew spiritual strength? We don't know precisely, but we can realize that Jesus knew the need and the power of prayer.

As a demonstration of His power with God, Jesus healed many who were diseased. Luke relates that Jesus touched a leper, telling him, "Be thou clean." He further charged the cleansed leper that he "tell no man." Yet, "So much the more went there a fame abroad of Him: and great multitudes came together to hear and to be healed by Him of their infirmities."[23] Accordingly, as His popularity virtually exploded, our Lord "...withdrew himself into the wilderness, and prayed."[24] Was it not His habit to do this?

With popularity came persecution on Jesus' journeys as He "came unto His own." For as He healed and helped, the Pharisees charged that He had desecrated the Sabbath: Jesus, by healing; His disciples, by plucking ears of corn. Accordingly, the Pharisees were "filled with madness" and plotted His destruction. It was during this time of turmoil that Jesus "went out into a mountain to pray, and continued there all night in prayer to God."[25]

During the first six months of His last year of earthly ministry, prayers attended four major events.

First, all of the gospel accounts mention prayer at the feeding of the 5,000.[26] Luke is most specific in relating that Jesus blessed "them" (the five loaves and the two fishes).[27] John tells that the miracle brought the instant sheep-like following; for "when Jesus therefore perceived that they would come and take him by force, to make Him a King, He departed into a mountain alone."[28] Matthew tells us that He went apart "to pray."[29] By thus retreating to his "prayer closet," Jesus evaded the "Devil's Triangle": the lust of the flesh (food), the lust of the eye (a kingdom), and the pride of life (pomp and power).[30]

Second, at the feeding of the 4,000, Jesus gave thanks first for the bread and then for the fish.[31] In so doing, Jesus demonstrated specificity in expressing gratitude.

"Whether therefore ye eat, or drink, or whatsoever ye do, do all to the glory of God."[32] For as Paul admonished the saints at Thessalonica, "In every thing give thanks."[33]

Third, despite His miracles of mercy and the tenderness of His teaching, Jesus' popularity waned under increasing persecution. Many had already left Him "and walked no more with Him."[34] Indeed, there was the possibility that the very apostles themselves would leave, for Jesus asked the twelve, "Will you also go away?"[35] Thus, before he faced the apostles, He faced God. For Luke states that He "was alone praying...all night."[36] The next day, he asked those who "knew" Him best, "Whom say ye that I am?" Simon Peter answered, "THOU ART THE CHRIST, THE SON OF THE LIVING GOD." Then, Jesus answered him, "Blessed art thou, Simon Barjona: for flesh and blood hath not revealed it unto thee, but my Father which is in heaven."[37] Realizing that the apostles could also go away, did not Jesus ask to be revealed to His apostles as the Christ? Was it not Jesus' prayer power that brought this special and timely revelation?

Fourth, Jesus prayed before His transfiguration. Matthew states simply that He took Peter, James, and John into a high mountain "and was transfigured."[38] Luke directly reveals the impact of Jesus' prayer power; for Luke states that *"as He prayed,* the fashion of His countenance was altered, and His raiment was white and shining."[39] In those miraculous moments, Elijah and Moses appeared and talked with Jesus about His approaching crucifixion in Jerusalem. The sleeping apostles awoke and beheld His glory. Whereupon, Peter envisioned a tabernacle for worshipping each of the three spiritual giants. However, a cloud covered them, and there came a voice out of the cloud saying, "This is my beloved Son: hear Him."[40] When the cloud had passed, Jesus was alone! Was it not the prayer power of Jesus that evoked the change in His countenance and the ultimate heavenly injunction: **"hear him"**?

The Final Six Months

The first record of the words of Jesus' prayers are first found in the final six months of His ministry.

Upon hearing the report of the seventy He had sent forth as "lambs among wolves"[41] Jesus rejoiced in spirit, and said,

> *"I thank thee; O father of heaven and earth, that thou has hid these things from the wise and prudent, and hast revealed them unto babes: even so, Father; for so it seemed good in thy sight. All things are delivered to me of my father: and no man knoweth who the Father is, but the Son, and he to whom the Son will reveal Him."*[42]

Even as the time came for His deliverance up into heaven, "He steadfastly set His face to go to Jerusalem."[43] Accordingly, He had sent out seventy who would "carry neither purse nor scrip, nor shoes."[44] Then, when they returned with joy, saying, "Lord, even the devils are subject unto us through thy name,"[45] was it not by prayer power that they could gain such victory? On the occasion when the disciples tried and failed to heal a man's lunatic son, Jesus performed the miracle and instructed the apostle that "this kind goeth not out but by prayer and fasting."[46]

The disciples had repeatedly witnessed the accomplishment of the impossible by the prayers of Jesus! Hence, as He was praying, one of His disciples asked Him, **"Lord, teach us to pray."**[47] Accordingly, He uttered what has come to be known as "the Lord's Prayer." More properly, however, it is the disciple's prayer wherein Jesus called for

ADORATION   "Hallowed be thy name";

CONFESSION   "Forgive us our sins, for we also
                           forgive every one that is
                           indebted to us."

THANKSGIVING   "Thine is the kingdom, and the
                           power and the glory, forever.
                           Amen."

SUPPLICATION   "Thy will be done. Give us this
                           day our dailybread. Lead us
                           not into temptation; but deliver
                           us from evil."[48]

As Jesus stated the major functions or A C T S of prayer, He taught the manner of prayer. Accordingly, He warned against vain repetition in public and prescribed instead prayer in secret, in the privacy of one's closet, with the Lord God alone.[49] He further illustrated that asking is consonant with importunity (urgent and persistent begging).[50] As a child comes to trust an earthly father, so too the pray-er learns to depend upon the heavenly Father to give the best gifts.[51]

Jesus realized that because of His oneness with the Father, He would give the very best gifts, including life itself. Upon hearing of the death of His dear friend Lazarus, Jesus delayed His coming. Was it not so that he could pray to God that Lazarus be resurrected upon command? Was not the implication of His prayer at the tomb of Lazarus:

"Father, I thank thee that thou has heard me. And I know that thou hearest me always: but because of the people which stand by I said it, that they may believe that thou hast sent me. And when He had thus spoken, He cried with a loud voice, 'Lazarus, come forth.'"[52]

Truly, Jesus demonstrated by raising the dead that nothing is too hard for the Lord God.[53]

Jesus did not restrict His tender touch to embracing one raised from the dead. Despite the rebuke by His disciples to the parents for bringing their infants to be touched and prayed for, Jesus blessed the children and said to His disciples, "Suffer little children and forbid them not to come unto me for such is the kingdom of heaven."[54] Jesus went even further to reinforce the innocence of children by echoing His admonition to His disciples who argued as to which of them should be greatest in the kingdom of heaven. For he answered that none of them would be until each was converted -- in HEART, MIND, AND SOUL -- and become as little children.[55] Thus, He cautioned, "Verily I say unto you, 'Whosoever shall not receive the kingdom of God as a little child shall in no wise enter therein.'"[56]

The teacher of humility clothed Himself with it. For as He arrived as the lamb to be slaughtered in Jerusalem, certain Greeks came and said, "Sir, we would see Jesus."[57] Whereupon, Jesus presented the inescapable analogy that pointed to His humiliating crucifixion when He answered:

"The hour is come that the son of man should be glorified. Verily, verily, I say unto you, 'Except a corn of wheat fall into the ground and die, it abideth alone: but if it die it bringeth forth much fruit.'"[58]

Then in order that they might truly see Jesus, He prayed. "Father, glorify thy name."[59] Consequently, there came a voice from heaven, saying, "I have glorified it, and will glorify it again."[60]

Shortly thereafter, Jesus demonstrated His humility by washing the feet of His disciples and praying for them. Six times He uttered the promise of prayer power: "Whatsoever ye shall ask in my name, that will I do, that the Father may be glorified in the Son."[61] Then, because He knew that the Lord God truly answers prayers, He interceded first for Himself, "Father...glorify thy Son, that thy Son also may glorify thee."[62] Then He pleaded on behalf of His immediate apostles, "I have manifested thy name unto the men which thou gavest them me: and they have kept thy word...I pray for them: I pray not for the world, but for them which thou hast given me; for they are thine."[63] Yet, this was in no way a spiritually myopic plea, for Jesus saw many future disciples. And so He prayed not "for these alone but for them also which shall believe in me through thy word; **that they may all be one: As Thou, Father, art in me and I in Thee,** that they may also be one in us: that the world may believe that thou hast sent me."[64] Truly, this was "the Lord's Prayer" wherein He prayed for Himself and for all disciples who would come unto Him and learn that He is meek and lowly, His yoke is easy and his burden is light.[65]

The prayers of Jesus at the Last Supper were in preparation for His passion and for all who would follow Him. Thus, as He first took bread and then of the cup and "blessed" each of these in turn, He asked His apostles to die with Him. For as He prophesied that His body would be broken for them and His blood would be shed for them, He invited them to "eat" and to "drink." This they did, for their following Him and "doing this in remembrance" of Him ultimately led to their own deaths. Justin Martyn's <u>Book of Martyrs</u> traces each of their ministries to their being boiled in oil, flayed to death, crucified, beheaded, or to being exiled. Is the servant above his master? As the early Christians met together upon every first day of the week to eat the bread and drink the cup,[66] was not persecution ever fresh before them so that they drank to their deaths? **Can the child of God do less today if he is to drink worthily?**[67]

Realizing the awfulness of His betrayal even during the moments of His prayers at the Last Supper, He led his apostles out with a song and into the Garden of Gethsemane where He learned obedience and gained the strength He needed through prayer. As He crossed over the Cedron Brook and went on alone, He experienced "trouble in His soul."[71] Three times He prayed, because of His terror of the cross. Yet, his words were not "vain repetition," for his sweat came as drops of blood.[72] He was in His own prayer closet, in secret with God alone, begging for a complete surrender of His own will. Truly the words of a song are correct, "Oh, what a wondrous love I see, freely shown for you and me when He suffered there alone."

Prayer in the garden brought strength of resolve to the one who prayed. Yet, since only Jesus prayed, others were not spiritually strong when the betrayers came "with swords and staves."[73] Peter, for example, was without the armament of prayer power though he was willing to go to prison and to die with Jesus. Peter's preparation, however, was to strap on a sword and when the time came, to strike down the first accuser he could find. When Jesus lovingly rebuked him, he stood exposed and stripped of all human resources. Thus, he fled along with the others who had not maintained their prayer watch.[74]

Satan wanted all to follow him, but especially Simon Peter. For Jesus looked tenderly and said, "Simon, Simon, Satan hath desired to have you, that he may sift you as wheat; **but I have prayed for thee:** and when thou art converted, strengthen the brethren."[75] Later, when Peter had been tried with fire and had come forth with faith more precious than gold,[76] he could admonish the holy priesthood: **"Watch unto prayer."**[77]

Although Jesus continued instant in prayer, his death brought darkness over the entire earth for the space of three hours and a sense of failure in prayer power. For He cried with a loud voice, "My God, My God, why hast thou forsaken me."[78] Until that time, His every prayerful utterance had been on behalf of others,

FOR HIS ENEMIES:	"Father forgive them for they know not what they do."[79]
FOR HIS MOTHER:	To Mary: "Woman, behold thy son."[80] To John: "Behold thy mother."[81]
FOR A THIEF:	In response to the request: "Remember me when thou comest into thy kingdom," He said, "Verily I say unto thee, today thou shalt be with me in paradise."[82]

Later, out in the darkness, He had not strength left to intercede, except for Himself, and all He could do was realize the triumph of His earlier plea, "Not my will but thine be done." For he cried loudly, "Father, into my hands I commend my spirit."[83]

Death on the cross was not the end as those on the road to Emmaus had supposed. For as the stranger who joined them for the evening meal led the prayer, they realized what had happened. They knew what others can know by faith to this day: **Jesus is the Christ the son of the living God.**[84] Hence, He gained the victory over sin and over death by his PRAYER POWER. For as Hebrews affirms, "When He had offered up prayers and supplications with strong crying and tears unto Him that was able to save Him from death, He was heard in that He feared."[85]

His PRAYER POWER continues today without limit:

> *"He is able also to save them to the uttermost that come unto God by Him, seeing that He ever liveth to make intercession for them."*[86]

He Ended In Prayer

The last public appearance during Jesus' earthly ministry was on a mountain in Bethany at His ascension. Luke is vividly descriptive of Jesus' last moments on earth:

> *"And He led them out as far as Bethany, and He lifted up His hands and blessed them. And it came to pass, while He blessed them, He was parted from them, and carried up into heaven."*[18]

In essence, Jesus was interceding for others even as He ascended into heaven.

Let us be assured that Jesus has not ceased making intercession. Recall, for example, that as Stephen was preaching salvation through the death, burial and resurrection of Jesus, he gazed steadfastly into heaven. As he prayed, did he not see that crucified and risen Savior pleading for him? For as Stephen saw heaven open and beheld the glory of God, he beheld Jesus standing on the right hand of God.[19] Was it not because of Stephen's prayer power that he could see Jesus interceding and could also pray as the Savior had done, upon the cross, "Lord, lay not this sin to their charge."[20] For as Hebrews reveals, "He is able to save them to the uttermost that come unto God by Him, seeing that **He ever lives to intercession for them.**"[21]

Child of God, come to pray as did Jesus, the prince of pray-ers: "not my will, but thine, be done."[87] Then you will know as did the unknown author of the following poem:

> "With eager heart, and will on fire,
> I sought to win my great desire.
> 'Peace shall be mine' I said. But life
> Grew bitter in the endless strife.
>
> My soul was weary, and my pride
> Was wounded deep. To heaven I cried:
> 'God give me peace, or I must die.'
> The dumb stars glittered no reply.
>
> Broken at last, I bowed my head
> Forgetting all myself, and said:
> 'Whatever comes, His will be done'
> And in that moment, peace was won."

STOP

Chapter VII

ATTAINING WISDOM IN PRAYER POWER

> "Wisdom is the principal thing; therefore, get wisdom; and
> with all thy getting, get understanding."
> -Proverbs 4:7

Surprise! Surprise! Surprise!

As a constant and somewhat irritating reminder, Gomer
Pyle has often pointed out to people that the unexpected
has happened. Thus, it does, for God's answers are full of
surprises that are often dumbfounding and dispiriting.
For example, in his short story entitled "Blackberry
Winter," Robert Penn Warren describes the sad state of
"Ole Jebb" who in his youth had prayed, "Lord, just give
me my strength for to endure." Hence, he found himself
as a very old and very sad person, for he had outlived his
wife and all of their children as well as all of his life-long
friends. Thus, he wept, "The Lord gave me my strength to
endure. But now he has left me all alone. A person just
doesn't know what to pray for -- being only human."

Setting Aside Stumbling Blocks

Solomon advised, "Wisdom is the principal thing;
therefore get wisdom: and with all thy getting get
understanding."[1] This wisdom and understanding must
be from God, for "God's ways are not man's ways."[2] The
wisdom of God is foolishness to man. Yet, even the
foolishness of God is wiser than the best wisdom of man.[3]
Hence, it is essential that the prayer warrior strive for the

wisdom that is from above that is *"pure, peaceable, gentle, easy to be entreated, full of good fruits, without hypocrisy, and without partiality."*[4]

Though the wisdom of God appears easily attainable ("all you gotta' do is ask"),[5] it is not. It requires a search as for silver and gold. Accordingly, one must cry out and lift up the voice in total surrender to His will.[6] Otherwise, prayers become powerless, and the powerless pray-ers cease to pray.

Lack of Faith

When Philip preached Jesus, the consequence was that the Ethiopian knew he needed to be baptized to receive the forgiveness of his sins. Hence, when they came to a body of water, the Ethiopian said, "See, here is water. What doth hinder me to be baptized?" Whereupon, the evangelist gave the condition: "If thou believest with all thine heart, thou mayest."[7] In exactly the same way, prayer must be in faith, without any doubting; for he that "wavereth is like a wave of the sea driven with the wind and tossed." This poor pray-er must not even think that he will receive any thing of the Lord.[8]

Prayer without faith is prayer without power. For it is not prayer *per se* that changes things but the "prayer of faith."[9]

Time and again, Jesus stressed the vitalness of faith:

> *"According to your faith be it unto you."*[10]
> *"Thy faith hath saved thee, go in peace."*[11]
> *"If you have faith and doubt not...it shall be done."*[12]

On one occasion, for example, Jesus used a grain of mustard seed, the smallest seeds, to illustrate that even the least quantity of unfaltering faith could move mountains.

Many today are fond of adding initials after their names to establish greater credibility: M.D., Ph.D., *et cetera.* Let the prayer warrior learn in Christ's school of prayer to add two letters: M.M. - MOUNTAIN MOVER.

Selfishness

A Christian lady related how she had prayed successfully for six successive jobs only to find each in turn worse than the previous one. Finally, she came to realize that it was just for herself that she had prayed. So, in realizing that she had prayed "amiss" that she might consume it upon her own lusts,[13] she prayed for a seventh job but this time that she might use it to glorify God thereby. Tears of joy welled in her eyes as she described the new job as "fantastic, beyond my dreams."

Prayers must reach beyond the self. For even unselfish petitions may become self-centered. The showers of God's blessing do give life and blossoms to each flower of the field. Yet, the one whose primary concern is "myself alone" can become one of a special strain identifiable as a blooming idiot.

Perhaps, the best antidote for selfishness in all of its poisonous varieties is the development of a genuine concern for others culminating in intercessory prayer. As has been expressed in a poem-song entitled:

"Others"

"Lord, help me live from day to day in such a self-forgetful way that even when I kneel to pray, my prayer shall be for others."

Rejecting God's Best Answers

How often do the prayer answers of God seem to defy human logic! For example, the Israelites saw starvation ahead as they plunged into the Sinai desert region. Their new-found freedom did not prevent their poisonous invective: "Would to God we had died...in Egypt."[14] "Even as God caused the "bread of heaven" to become their daily banquet, they rejected His best blessings.

As the people continued to murmur against God, He yielded to the will of men and gave them meat for thirty consecutive days. Yet, the "wisdom of man" demonstrated his own foolishness. For the anger of the Lord was kindled against them: and those that originally lusted were killed "while the flesh was yet between their teeth."[15] Others who lived were filled with "leanness of soul."[16]

Oh, that each child of God could learn how to deal with his desires as did the apostle Paul. Because of his "thorn in the flesh," Paul besought the Lord three times that He would remove it. Consider Paul's attentive ear in listening expectantly for God's wise answer. For although God did not do exactly as Paul had requested, He gave a better answer: *"My grace is sufficient."*[17]

Some have contended that God said, "No," to Paul, thereby suggesting that because God did not He would not remove Paul's thorn in the flesh. Yet, was it not that Paul accepted God's wisdom rather than accept the lesser blessing -- which he could have had with incessant begging? After all, did He not Himself by prayer power remove a myriad of thorns in the flesh from many others?

Truly, Paul was able to count it all joy as he learned that his faith worked patience unto her perfect work.[18] Could he not more fully realize the truth of his own teaching to the Corinthian Christians, "God hath chosen the weak things of the world to confound the things of the mighty?"[19] Could he not most gladly glorify in infirmity, that the power of Christ might rest upon him?[20]

Impatience With God

"Lord, give me patience, and give it to me now," demonstrates the desperate demands of some who would insist upon telling God when and how to answer. Yet, the prayer warrior must leave time and circumstance to God.

Matthew Henry once said, "God's providences often seem to contradict His purposes, even when they are serving them, and working at a distance towards the accomplishment of them."

Joseph learned to trust in God, for things are not what they seem. He had surely prayed for the fulfillment of the vision that his brothers would bow before him "as sheaves of grain."[21] Yet, how could he have known that the way to the fulfillment of God's plan and purpose would witness attempted murder, slavery, attempted rape, and false imprisonment? How could he have known that it would take more than *twenty years* to witness God's grace in his life? Even so, Joseph trusted not in appearances but in the providence of God. For when his brothers finally bowed before him, he said, "So now it was not you that sent me hither, but God."[22]

Moses' impatient striking of the rock with his prayer rod -- because the water did not flow *immediately* -- caused God to be angry and to punish Moses. Things are not what they seem -- trust in God as to when and how his unfailing promise to answer will come.

Lack of Priorities

"Be ye holy, for I am holy,"[23] states the Lord God. Hence, the penitent prays, "Lord make me holy." The conditions in the pray-er's life deteriorate to "Lord, improve my circumstances." The person may well sense a contradiction, for he has asked for one thing and God depicts a dilemma of a different sort. Can we not hear Him ask, "Which do you want, holiness or comfort and ease?" Does He not urge that each child of God, "establish priorities," sending, first of all, holiness, realizing that He will add other things?[24] Does not the wise person realize that God's priorities are established as a means of perfecting the saints?

Failure to establish priorities according to His will may lead to another set of apparent contradictions. For example, two Christians pray for the same job, the only one available. Again, the minister prays, "Help me to keep this ministry," while the elders pray, "Lord, help us find a new minister." Obviously, only one of the two options is open in each case. After all, God can hardly answer both, can He?

The answer is, "Yes! He can!" **Nothing is too hard for the Lord.**[25] Yet, it would be impractical at times for God to say, "Yes." The creation of a second job might result in little work for both applicants. Otherwise, the minister's staying on might result in loss of greater opportunities elsewhere. Thus, the establishment of priorities is essential by the person's prayer for wisdom and vision to see the best possibilities.

Pride in Piety

When the Lord gives His best blessings, the pray-er may become lifted in his own eyes, for he has "wrestled with God"[26] and prevailed. Surely, the Pharisee who went to the temple to pray was grateful that the Lord had heard his prayers and had helped him to avoid committing adultery, perpetrating extortion, or being unjust. He realized gratitude for God's perfecting through fasting and through tithing. Yet, because God had blessed him by these marvelous means the Pharisee had need of nothing. Ironically, in God's eyes he had need of everything because of his "holier than thou"[27] disposition.

The pray-er must not assume that prayer power is inherent in the person who prays but in the Lord God Himself. Ezekiel tells of a tree that flourished boastfully beside a river until the river changed its course. The death of the tree depicts not only the dethroning and the death of a king but also that God is the King of Kings and Lord of Lords.[28]

One of the most successful pray-ers was King Hezekiah who was able even to change the will of God. For the prophet Isaiah had said, "Thus saith the Lord, 'Set thine house in order; for thou shalt die, and not live.'"[29] Because Hezekiah could remind God of his goodness, with much the same phrasing as that of the Pharisee, he was able to ask for and be granted change of the will of God. For he received fifteen additional years to live.[30]

Despite even the accompanying sign of the sun going back ten degrees, Hezekiah "rendered not again according to the benefit done unto him; for his heart was lifted up."[31] Because Hezekiah forgot the true source of prayer power -- the Lord God Himself -- consequently, God poured His wrath upon Hezekiah as well as upon the people he governed. Nonetheless, when "Hezekiah humbled himself for the pride of his heart," the Lord heard his prayers and helped him and those he prayed for as well.[32]

Lack of Fervency

Someone once referred to baptism as a "ritual," something that one does to please God. In the same breath, the person included prayer as a "ritual." Yet, prayer must become ever so much more than as a demonstration for others to witness one's actions that merely follow a prescribed form. The value of such vanity is no greater than that of the goldfish: to be seen of men. For what other value was there to the long-winded public prayers of the Pharisees than to be seen of men?

The purpose for undertaking prayer is not to impress but to approach God. Thus, there must be fervency in spirit[33] as one comes "boldly before the throne to find grace to help in time of need."[34]

Paul stated that he would pray with the spirit and with the understanding.[35] Hence, he could pour out his heart's desire in a selfless soul-emptying way.[36]

Jesus tells of a widow who begged the favor of a judge who "feared not God and regarded not man."[37] Yet, even the unjust judge granted her request because of the fervency of her petition. Then Jesus asks, "And shall not God avenge His own elect, which cry day and night unto Him, though He bear long with them?"[38]

Jesus urged that His followers "faint not in prayer."[39] Accordingly, the early church continued steadfastly in prayer.[40] For just as we know that "faint heart never wins fair maid" so, too, faint heart never gets God's grace. Indeed, "We shall reap if we faint not."[41]

Unforgiven Sins

Fervency will be to no avail so long as the pray-er fails to repent of all sins in his life. The Psalmist said, "If I regard iniquity in my heart, the Lord will not hear me."[42]

Thus, Isaiah, after offering assurance of God's power, issued the same warning:

> *"Behold the Lord's hand is not shortened that it cannot save nor His ear heavy that He cannot hear: But our iniquities have separated between you and your God, and your sins have hid His face from you, that He will not hear."*[43]

Thus, sin becomes an impenetrable barrier no matter how fervent the prayer.

One may argue, however, that it would be impossible to confess every sin. First, there are too many sins for one to confess. Second, the sinner may not know all of his own sins anyway. Yet, if the person remains "instant in prayer,"[44] it becomes easy to keep wiping the slate clean. In so doing, the sinner increases his threshold of sensitivity to and awareness of the need for forgiveness. For sins done "out of ignorance," the Christian who "meditates in His law day and night"[45] will have few areas he doesn't know about and can still prayerfully ask forgiveness of even these few. Thus, the sinner learns wisdom in casting aside "the weight of sin that doth so easily beset."[46]

Wasted Words

The story teller says, "Stop me if you've heard this one before." And because the Lord God will in the day of judgment require each person to give an account of every idle word,[47] let the "storyteller" in prayer avoid heaping up "vain repetitions" expecting God to enjoy long speeches.[48] Rather, let the child of God begin with the comforting assurance that the Father already knows, already cares, and has already planned His answer. For as the Lord told Isaiah, "I am sought of them that ask not for me; I am found of them that sought me not."[49]   "It shall come to pass, that before they call, I will answer; and while they are yet speaking, I will hear."[50]

Words become wasted often because the child of God has waited until it is too late. For simplicity, imagine the student who takes a standardized exam and prays only after the exam to pass. Consider also the prospective heir who begs that his already-dead uncle will remember him in his will. Or pity the poor person terminated for excessive absences due to alcoholism who prays not to be fired.

The basic problem is that the person has not continued "instant in prayer," ever alert to needs before they reach crisis proportions. A falling rock creates an avalanche when other rocks are also loosened. Thus, prayer power requires maintenance of constant communication with the solid Rock of Ages.

A Clear Path

A heart-broken Christian comes to a counselor to confess fault and to ask for prayers. To be sure, this is a scriptural method of solving the problem.[51] Yet, is it not also the case that the first fault requiring crisis intervention is that the child of God did not pray?

But why? Has not every child of God the same access to the Father through Jesus the Son?

What, then, are the excuses -- the stumbling blocks? "I didn't feel like praying" may well cover a lack of faith, selfishness, rejection of God's best answer, impatience with God, lack of priorities, pride in piety, lack of fervency, unforgiven sins, wasted words, or some other excuse. The fervently effectual pray-er must remove the stumbling blocks so as to have a clear path to the goal of the high calling in Christ Jesus.

Problems will come. As Job wisely spoke, "Man that is born of woman is but a few days and full of trouble."[52] Yet, one learns to pray without ceasing in an effort to trust God's true wisdom. Then, SURPRISE! SURPRISE! SURPRISE! The wisdom will come.[53] The path will be clear all the way home with God.

REMEMBER:

S T O P   ENGAGE IN **S**PECIFIC
                    TIMES
                    OF
                    PRAYER

A C T S   Your **A**dorations,
                    Confessions,
                    Thanksgivings and
                    Supplications will
                    change your life and
                    the world around you.

It has been well stated,

"More things are wrought by prayer than this world dreams of."   For "the Lord pities those who fear Him.   For He knows our frame; He remembers that we are dust."[54]

Chapter VIII

INCREASING PRAYER POWER THROUGH FASTING

> "I humbled my soul with fasting; and my prayer returned into mine own bosom."   -Psalms 35:13

When You Fast

Unquestionably, the greatest sermon ever preached was by the Lord Jesus Christ in what is traditionally referred to as the "Sermon on the Mount."[1] Not only because of the identity of the preacher, but because of the message that breathes pure wisdom, others have drawn more sermons from it than any other basic portion of scripture. For out of it are indeed the issues of life.

Having been a Christian for 47 years, this writer has heard countless "Sermon on the Mount" lessons concerning virtually every subject except one: namely -- FASTING. Yet, Jesus stated explicitly, "When ye (all of you) fast"[2] and "when thou (as an individual) fastest."[3] The presumption of modern-day preaching has been that *if* you fast, you will follow Jesus' instruction in doing so. Yet, the word Jesus used each time in reference to fasting was not **if** but **when**. Thus, does not Jesus anticipate that true believers will practice fasting, individually and collectively?   The parallel phrasing Jesus used to introduce the manner of giving, of praying, and of fasting is inescapable. **"When thou doest thine alms," "When thou prayest," and "When thou fastest,"**[4] all seem to suggest that *followers* of Christ *will* give, *will* pray, *will* fast.

On another occasion and also very early in His ministry, Jesus' disciples came unto Him and asked why His disciples were not then practicing -- fasting as did the Pharisees and the followers of John the Baptist. His answer began with an allegorical question, "Can the children of the bride chamber fast, while the bridegroom is with them?"[5] In so doing, He was asking, "Can you believers of me, the bridegroom, fast while I am still with you?" Yet, He prophesied of the days when He would be "taken away from them, and then shall they fast in those days."[6] Was this not an unequivocal reference to the time after His ascension and throughout the existence of the church?

Fasting was a recurrent theme not only in the precepts of Jesus but in His practice of prayer power as well. For as He prepared Himself for increasingly difficult decisions, His prayer was not without fasting. When He came, for example, in prayer for baptism by John, the Holy Spirit *immediately afterwards* drove Him into the wilderness to be tempted of Satan.[7] One may reasonably infer that Jesus continued in prayer for the entire 40 days of His trial. For the Holy Spirit directive to all saints is to ask God for wisdom when "ye fall into diverse temptations."[8] But why should Jesus also fast for forty days? Was it not so that He could thereby increase His prayer power with God?

From Strength To Strength

At the time of His Baptism, it would have seemed that Jesus was at the height of human and divine strength. For the miraculous revelation was made as the heavens were opened and the Spirit of God descended like a dove and lighted upon Jesus and a voice from Heaven declared. "This is my beloved Son, in whom I am well pleased."[9]

Despite the divine declaration accompanied by signs and wonders, the humanity of Jesus needed greater strength still to wrestle against "powers and principalities, against the rulers of the darkness of this world, against spiritual wickedness in high places."[10] Thus, fasting "buffeted" Jesus' body to bring it unto subjection of the spirit.[11] Thus, as Satan came to Him with no holds barred throughout the period of forty days, Jesus was able to out-wrestle the prince of the powers of this world.[12] Moreover, at the end of the forty-day fast, when the body was at its weakest point, Satan launched his most devastating assault. He asked Jesus to perform a miracle to cause the pangs of hunger to subside. Having failed in this, Satan called upon Jesus to end all of the pain of His body by attempting a suicide plunge from the pinnacle of the Temple, assuring Jesus that angels would catch Him before He reached the craggy rocks below. Once again thwarted in his efforts to overcome Jesus, Satan resorted to offering Jesus rulership over all the glorious kingdoms of the world. Yet, because Jesus had undergone spiritual strengthening attained through prayer with fasting, He demonstrated the strength of His meditation by answering,

> *"It is written, Thou shalt worship the Lord thy God, and Him only shalt Thou serve."*[13]

Because Jesus escaped the "Devil's Triangle": the lust of the flesh, the lust of the eye, and the pride of life,[14] the devil left Him, and angels came and ministered unto Him.[15]

When Jesus was in heaven, He had inherent and unfailing strength without diminution. But, when He became flesh and dwelt among us, He lived with two basic strengths as do all humans: physical and spiritual.[16] Because of the constant war between these two aspects of each person,[17] it is necessary for the spiritual to be dominant.[18] By the flesh shall no man prevail with God "for if ye live after the flesh, ye shall die: but if ye through the Spirit do mortify the deeds of the body, ye shall live."[19]

Fasting is the voluntary giving up of doing something good for the body in order to do something better in the spirit. Later in this chapter, one will find application of this principle to all areas of one's life. At present, however, discussion will focus upon the more restrictive application of scripture -- voluntarily abstaining from eating food (doing something good for the body) in order to strengthen the spiritual man. For example, during the Medo-Persian captivity of the Jews, the chief advisor to King Ahasuerus, one Haman, bribed the king with $3,000,000 in order to exterminate all of the Jews. By the providence of God, however, a Jewess named Esther served as his queen. Because of her great love for her own people, she asked that all of the Jews fast (abstain from food and drink) for three days. Was it not because of her fasting (with prayer?) that gave her courage to offer her life for her people, emboldening her to say, "So will I go in unto the king, which is not according to the law; and if I perish, I perish."[20]

During that same captivity, a priest named Ezra used fasting with prayer to increase the strength of himself and his companions. For after King Artaxerxes had declared that certain priests could return to Jerusalem to rebuild the temple of God,[21] Ezra stated,

> *"I was ashamed to require of the king a band of soldiers and horsemen to help us against the enemy in the way because we had spoken unto the king, saying, 'The hand of our God is upon all them for good that seek Him; but His power and His wrath is against all them that forsake*

Him.' ***SO WE FASTED AND BESOUGHT***
OUR GOD FOR THIS: *And he was intreated*
of us."[22]

And so, these priests of God increased their trust to walk
without their own physical strength or even that of
soldiers. With what result? Ezra exclaims that "the hand
of God was upon us, and He delivered us from the hand of
the enemy, and of such as lay in wait by the way."[23]

The virtue of fasting with prayer in the undergoing of
pain was not simply for punishment of the body. The
Bible declares time and again that the primary function
of fasting was for the humbling of the soul before God.
When David was forced to flee as a fugitive from his
throne, he cried, "My clothing was sackcloth: I
**HUMBLED MY SOUL WITH FASTING: AND MY
PRAYER RETURNED INTO MINE OWN BOSOM."**[24]

When the plague of locusts came as a "nation without
number" and laid waste all crops of the field,[25] the
prophet Joel instructed priests and ministers to "sanctify
ye a fast...and cry unto the Lord"[26] in order that every
person might turn to Him with "all your heart."[27] Thus
was resounded a clear echo of the promise of God, to King
Solomon,

> *"If I shut up heaven that there be no rain, or **IF I***
> ***COMMAND THE LOCUSTS TO DEVOUR***
> ***THE LAND,*** *or if I send pestilence among my*
> *people; if my people which are called by my*
> *name shall **HUMBLE THEMSELVES AND***
> ***PRAY,*** *and seek my face, and turn from their*
> *wicked ways; then will I hear from heaven, and*
> *will forgive their sin and will heal their land."*[28]

Was not then the "humbling" a matter of fasting?

Instructions for observance of the Day of Atonement focused primarily upon afflicting the souls.[29] Celebration was to be by "convocation" (*calling upon the Lord in prayer*) and by fasting. Accordingly, when Luke described the sailing against "contrary" winds that endangered the lives of all aboard, he relates that Paul spent the time in prayer and fasting, having delayed his warning until "the fast" (the Day of Atonement) was past.[30]

The ministry of Paul was apostolic and thus was Holy Spirit inspired and Christ-led. Yet, he fasted with prayer thereby humbling himself and passing "from (physical) strength to (spiritual) strength."[31] He did not boast of this "to be seen of men."[32] But he did defend his ministry against carping and corrupting Corinthians. In so doing, he demonstrated how he would not glory "after the flesh" but in "infirmities."[33] Hence, as should be anticipated, Paul was in (prayer) "watchings often" and "in fastings often."[34]

Coping With Crises

Special problems require special solutions. And so, the scripture shows how prayer with fasting brought sufficient increase of spiritual strength that the Lord was able to use for successfully coping with whatever crisis existed at the time. Jesus was able to defeat the devil's most terrible temptations. Esther was thus enabled to avert annihilation of her people. Ezra thereby gained special protection for a perilous journey on his return from exile to rebuild the temple in Jerusalem. Joel was thus able to remove a plague of locusts that completely devastated the land. Paul was thereby sustained during perils of robbers; perils of his own countrymen; perils of the heathen; perils of the city; perils of the wilderness; perils of the sea; perils of false brethren.[35]

Many times, the righteous have been subjected to the most cruel circumstances. And, every time they have resorted to prayer with fasting, they have emerged victorious. For instance, certain sons of Beliel were unsuccessful in their attempt to commit sodomy upon a priest, but they settled instead for the rape and murder of the Levite's concubine. And when the Israelites attempted to avenge this awful deed, they lost 18,000 soldiers. Indeed, despite the righteousness of their cause and the counsel of God, they met defeat in battle every day until they had fasted with prayer. When the Lord had witnessed their humbling of the spirit, He turned defeat into unqualified victory.[36]

Elijah had known great victory through prayer power in defeating the prophets of Baal and in causing the heavens to give abundance of rain, thus ending three and a half years of drought. Even so, he had to flee for his very life. It was not until he had fasted forty days that the Lord led him forth to an uninterrupted series of victories, including the ultimate victory over death itself, being taken up of God in a whirlwind.[37]

The irrevocable decree that anyone who prayed to any God or to any man sent Daniel to be eaten of lions because Daniel "kneeled upon his knees three times a day and prayed and gave thanks before his God, as he did aforetime."[38] In this crisis, even the king himself fasted on behalf of Daniel because he loved him. And when Daniel was delivered safely from the den of lions, the would-be destructors of the righteous were themselves fed to the lions. The lesson was not lost on Daniel, for when he read of the prophesy of Jeremiah, he set his face "by prayer and supplications, with fasting"[39] to see the salvation of the Lord not only in his own age -- as the Lord had miraculously done -- but for all ages. The Lord showed him spiritual triumph until the end of time. And from crisis once again, the righteous have been blessed for all time by prayer with fasting.

Because of great wickedness, Ninevah became a city targeted for destruction by the Lord God of heaven. Yet, when Jonah preached repentance, "the people of Ninevah believed God and proclaimed a fast, and put on sackcloth, from the greatest of them to the least of them."[40] The king also decreed that every person "cry mightily unto God" and "turn every one from his evil way."[41] Thus, prayer with fasting caused God to change his mind and delay the ultimate destruction until a new day of evil nearly 200 years later.

The new-born church of Christ met every crisis with prayer power for they continued steadfastly in prayers.[42] And while a direct statement that they also fasted is not always made, such must have been the case. For example, the miraculous release of Peter from prison was without direct reference to fasting, though "prayer was made without ceasing of the church unto God for him."[43] Yet, may it not be reasonably inferred that they did not eat since the prayer of the church was "without ceasing?" Again, for example, notice that when Paul and Barnabas were undertaking their first peril-filled missionary journey they "fasted and prayed."[44] Indeed, the missionaries were persecuted and driven from Antioch to Iconium. From there they fled for their lives to Lystra where Paul was stoned and left for dead.[45] Moreover, when they ordained elders in every city they "prayed with fasting."[46] Yet, because such reference is not made upon every such perilous undertaking, may it not be reasonably inferred that prayer with fasting occurred with *each* crisis in the infancy of the church? May the thoughtful reader infer that because Paul was in "fastings often" that there was a direct correlation with each of the perils he had been through?[47] And may not such voluntary humbling of the soul give greater spiritual strength as individuals and the church through the ages cope with crises?

Fasting is by no means a meritorious act *per se*.[48] For justification is by the grace of God through Jesus Christ and not by works of men.[49] The Pharisee, for example, who routinely fasted "twice a week" saw his voluntary giving up of food as the epitome of holiness. Yet, he stood condemned.[50]

An Acceptable Fast

"To be seen of men" or even of God alone is not sufficient for blessing to be given for fasting. In Isaiah 58, the longest treatment of fasting in the sacred scriptures, the Israelites learned a bitter lesson: their fasting (with prayer?) not only went "unnoticed" by God but witnessed occasion for them to be especially condemned. They prayerfully pleaded:

> *"Why have we fasted...and you have not noticed it? Why have we humbled ourselves and you have not noticed?"*[51]

The Lord God showed them fasting was not in itself a meritorious act. His people stood condemned because

1. On the day of fasting they did as they pleased.
2. They exploited their workers.
3. Their fasting ended in finger pointing, malicious quarrels, and even physical fights.[52]

Then as a loving, caring father, the Lord God gave the characteristics of a fast acceptable to Him. Those who fasted would have their prayers heard if they used the fast:

1. To loose the claims of injustice.
2. To set the oppressed free.
3. To share their food with the hungry.
4. To provide shelter for the poor.[53]

Accordingly, the Lord God stated:

"Your light will shine in the darkness, and your night will become like the noonday. The Lord will guide you always, and he will satisfy your needs in a sun-scorched land and will strengthen your frame. You will be like a well-watered garden, like a spring whose waters never fail."[54]

Post-Biblical Fasting

After the inspired scriptures were completed, church leaders frequently commended fasting through their writings. Indeed, during the first hundred years of the church three leaders wrote entire books devoted exclusively to fasting: Tertullian, Clement of Alexandria, and James of Nisibis.[55] In addition, in 96 A.D., Clement of Rome associated fasting and humiliation in reviewing the fasts of Moses on Mount Sinai. Polycarp, friend of the apostle John and bishop of Smyrna, urged the Philippians to be "sober unto prayer and constant in fastings."[56]

The Didache exhorted its readers to pray for their enemies and to fast for the ones who persecuted them.[57]

Barnabas upon two occasions repeated the 40-day fasts of Moses on Mount Sinai. He encouraged fellow Christians to follow the precepts for fasting set forth in Isaiah 58:4-10.[58]

Herman and Diognetus taught that fasting was for the humbling of the soul.[59]

In 128 A.D., Aristides reported to the Emperor Hadrian that it was common for Christians to fast two or three days and to give the food to the poor.[60]

Tertullian in his book On Fasting (208 A.D.) posited that abstinence earns the favor of God and reconciles God to man. He encouraged fasting as a weapon to fight the worst evils.[61]

During the reformation period, fasting was promoted. John Calvin exposed the abominable fasting habits of the Catholic Church in his time. Because animal food was forbidden, choice delicacies in abundant supply were consumed in the pretense of fasting. He taught that fasting has no value unless it is accompanied by genuine repentance, humiliation, and sorrow in the presence of God. He maintained that Jesus did not abolish fasting but assigned it to periods of distress.[62]

Matthew Henry, Johnathan Edwards, John Wesley, David Brainard, William Bramwell, Charles G. Finney, and Andrew Murray, each practiced and preached that fasting ought to be an integral aspect of Christian living.[63]

American history abounds with special occasions of fasting. Even before they set sail for the new world, the pilgrims held three fasts: 1) when they sought refuge in Holland, 2) after they decided to sail to America, and 3) before they departed.[64] Upon arrival, their governor, William Bradford, ordered a fast because of an extended drought. During the Stamp Act altercation, the Burgesses of Virginia appointed a fast.[65]

Wars were occasions for fastings during early American history. During the Revolutionary War, Congress designated three days of fasting. John Adams proclaimed a national fast in the midst of the French-American conflict. In the War of 1814, Congress called all citizens to a day of prayer and fasting. Abraham Lincoln identified three separate days for humiliation.[66]

During more recent times, presidents of the United States have called the nation to specific days of prayer during crisis. However, none, it seems has deemed it appropriate to include fasting.

Subsequent to Prayer Power Seminars conducted by this writer, certain churches of Christ now regularly proclaim fasts upon important occasions -- for example, the appointment of elders, the undertaking of benevolent, and mission efforts. Recently, college campus groups of the churches of Christ across the nation conducted a 33-hour fast to provide clean water for over 30,000 people in Ghana, West Africa. Surely, these humblings of the soul will cause the Lord God to say:

"Arise, shine; for thy light is come, and the glory of the Lord is risen upon thee. For, behold, the darkness shall cover the earth, and gross darkness the people: but the Lord shall arise upon thee, and his glory shall be seen upon thee."[67]

CHAPTER IX

PRAYER POWER BATTLE PLAN

> "The weapons of our warfare are not carnal, but mighty through God to the pulling down of strongholds."   -II Corinthians 10:4

Getting Ready

Fred feels just fantastic as he carefully chooses each part of his newly acquired Christian armor[1]:

HELMET OF SALVATION

SHIELD OF FAITH

BREASTPLATE OF
RIGHTEOUSNESS

GIRDLE OF TRUTH

SWORD OF
THE SPIRIT

GOSPEL-OF-PEACE FOOTWEAR

He puts on "the whole armor of God"[2] and goes forth to defeat the devil. Unfortunately, Fred falls prey to the first flurries of Satan's fiery darts. As with many other Saints, Fred simply has not properly prepared for battle. He has underestimated the "wiles of the devil"[3] who walks about as a "roaring lion seeking whom he may devour."[4]

Frustrated with the feeling that God has failed him in time of need, Fred gives up on God. He thus becomes a casualty -- a tragic figure, for it would have been better for him not to have known the way of righteousness than after having known it to turn from the holy commandment.[5]

Fred is little more than an armor bearer. For he has failed to pray. Oh, he has uttered a few empty generalizations, but he is not really ready. He has not been

> *"...Praying always with all prayer and supplication in the Spirit, and watching thereunto with all perseverance and supplication for all saints."*[6]

The Lines Of Battle

Because the devil often appears as an angel of light able to deceive the very elect,[7] it seems essential to distinguish clearly between God and the Devil.

To some, the reality of **GOD** and the **DEVIL** remains hazy, for each remains an impersonal abstraction. To others, the perception of GOD is a slavish conformity to a list of "do goods": the response to the Devil, to "do evil." Neither description seems adequate if one is ever to realize true prayer power. If, however, "GOD" means "LOVE": and the "DEVIL" means "HATE," the Christian soldier has a way of learning of the real Lord God of heaven and earth. For the key to understanding true PRAYER POWER is to learn the way of the cross -- the lesson of LOVE versus HATE. The following sketch affords visual clarification of this concept:

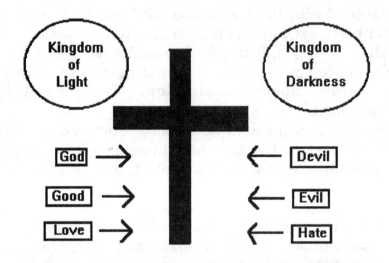

Accordingly, as one constantly claims prayer power, he learns the lesson of LOVE as Jesus went to the cross and died for us while we were yet his enemies.[8] In so doing, He gained victory over death and broke down the middle wall of partition: the handwriting of ordinances.[9] Because Jesus became flesh and dwelt among men,[10] His existence was a demonstrated reality, thereby making Him a personal Savior.

The battle lines have been clearly drawn. And the child of God must learn to become an effective warrior by learning how to LOVE -- by developing proper habits for prayer power to be actualized.

Acquiring Proper Prayer Habits

Mastery of an activity requiring physical skill demands rigorous training until the specific movements become ingrained. Much time, on a regular basis, must be devoted to develop good habits and to eliminate bad habits. So too, with prayer power -- where the child of God knows only constant victory -- is the result of acquisition of proper habits.

Designate Specific Times Of Prayer

A STOP sign appears in each chapter as a constant reminder that the pray-er must not squeeze in time for prayer. Rather, one must make time for prayer -- unhurried time, on at least a daily basis.

As the habit becomes settled, the attitude of prayer will not end with time spent in the closet of prayer. Thus, the child of God comes to "pray without ceasing"[11] in much the same way a "hacking" cough occurs spontaneously, always happening.

The designated time must be of sufficient duration so that the pray-er really communicates with God.

It will probably require setting aside at least fifteen minutes on a daily basis. However, a truly power-packed prayer watch will be of longer duration -- at least an hour a day.

It is not necessary that all of the time be at only one time. Indeed, David talked with God morning, noon and night.[12] Daniel set aside three times a day.[13] Indeed, so common was the practice of multiple times of daily prayer that the third hour,[14] the sixth hour,[15] and the ninth hour[16] became in the first century *Anno Domini* "hours of prayer."

Find A Private Place To Pray

When one establishes Specific Times of Prayer as a daily habit, it is a necessary corollary that one identify a specific location as well. Jesus instructed that each prayer have a "closet" where he can shut the door and pray to God in secret.[17]

One should choose the location as carefully as one chooses the time(s) of prayer. Within the structure of one's home, a room -- where possible -- ought to be set aside for prayer and relaxed devotionals. Where no "regular room" is available, a little imagination may be in order. One Christian, for example, now uses the "family room" for this purpose. Another has converted his garage into a place of prayer. Another has constructed a gazebo, a small room out in the back of the house. Still others, who are planning to build a house, are centering everything around the prayer room, referred to as "the gap."

"The gap" concept comes from Ezekiel where God calls for "...a man among them, that should stand in the gap before me in the land, that I should not destroy it: but I found none."[18] Does the Lord call today and find none who would stand in the gap and pray that the church of Christ will be victorious in the spiritual struggle with Satan?

When God found none to stand in "the gap," He poured out his indignation upon them.[19] Let every child of God truly stand in "the gap" and learn how to receive the "precious promises" attainable through prayer power.[20]

A Church That Prays

Wouldn't it be wonderful to be a member of a congregation where the name of every Saint was presented before the throne of grace every day? It happens when every child of God in a given congregation prays for himself. And indeed there is Biblical example and injunction that members of the Lord's church pray for each other.[21] Yet, in such cases, unless there is a systematic means of assuring that the names and needs of specific persons as well as those of the congregation are presented, many needs may be neglected. This suggests, at the very least, some semblance of organization for efficiency and efficacy.

"Hold on," someone says, "if Moses had waited to get organized, the Israelites would still be in the land of Goshen." Yet, it must be remembered that perhaps 2,000,000 people were able to clear the slave quarters within 24 hours. Surely, though we are not told how they were organized, may it not be reasonably inferred that *some kind* of organizing took place?

The specific methods for carrying out the initial marching orders were not the same once the Israelites were out into the Sinai desert. Even Moses had to learn how to organize the efforts of the "congregation." Turn to Exodus 18 and there read the advice of Jethro, Moses' father-in-law:

> *"Thou shalt provide out of all the people able men, such as fear God, men of truth hating covetousness; and place such over them, to be rulers of thousands, rulers of hundreds, rulers of fifties, and rulers of tens: and let them judge the people at all seasons."*[22]

Earlier, Jethro had observed people standing in line "from the morning unto the evening"[23] waiting to speak to Moses, "The thing that thou doest is not good. Thou wilt surely wear away, both thou, and this people that is with thee."[24] So, "Moses hearkened to the voice of his father-in-law, and did all that he had said."[25]

The early church also encountered problems that required systematic organization. For example, when the Grecian widows were being neglected in the daily ministration, seven men were set over this special task.[26] When Paul was taking up a special collection for the needy saints at Jerusalem, he instructed that all of the special collections be done upon each first Sunday so that there would be no collections when he came.[27]

Let's Get Organized

Every method herein suggested must be viewed as optional -- at the discretion of the elders of each congregation. May the wisdom of God be sought as you consider each recommendation:

1. Assignment of Names

How is it possible for every saint to be prayed for every day by at least one other Christian? One method is for every child of God willing to pray for others in the congregation on a daily basis to be given a list of names so as to include all members. The more volunteers there are the shorter each list will be, thereby increasing the chances for intimacy of relationships.

It is suggested that each intercessor make some effort to greet each person on his prayer list at every assembly. Should the person be absent, it would seem only natural to inquire as to the welfare of the person whose name he places before the throne of grace on a daily basis.

2. Prayer Papers

At a public assembly, a sheet (or sheets) of paper can be distributed for each member to write matters for which the entire congregation should pray. Because of the press of time, it may be well for each person to write only one request initially.

It is suggested that *equal* space on each sheet be provided for each of the major functions of prayer:

ADORATION

CONFESSION

THANKSGIVING

SUPPLICATION

Perhaps, the most convenient hour for allowing members to circulate the prayer power is during Bible classes each Lord's day morning.

The informality of the classroom setting suggests no loss of comfortability as members pass the prayer list from one to another. Moreover, the desires of the heart thus shared will reinforce the admonition to "pray without ceasing."[28]

Distribution of the prayer papers can be made as saints enter the building for the Lord's day evening service.

As a supplement to the prayer papers, a bulletin board could be placed in the foyer. Thus, as worshippers come and go, they could be further reminded to continue "instant in prayer."[29]

3. Brother's Keeper

Often a person is converted to Christ who has no relatives or close friends within the congregation. This "newborn babe"[30] will need special attention. The preacher and the elders can hardly be expected to provide the constant contact that must be maintained. Accordingly, mature Christians willing to undertake the responsibility for person-to-person relationships can be assigned to become a "brother's keeper," ministering to specific needs including becoming a companion in prayer.

There are other "singles" who could benefit immeasurably from a companion in prayer -- the unmarried, the widows, and the orphans. These special needs often become totally neglected. For everybody's business is nobody's business.

As companions in prayer, SPECIAL TIMES OF PRAYER may be structured so that the mutual bond of fellowship is strengthened thereby. The prayer warrior who makes time for prayer can continue the contact on a systematic basis. Mutual confession, intercession and supplication may thus be facilitated.

4. Prayer Groups

The history of the early church makes it evident that praying together is essential. In the face of severe persecution, the church came together and prayed. Luke describes the results:

> *"When they had prayed, the place was shaken where they were assembled together and they were all filled with the Holy Ghost and they spoke the word of God with boldness.*[31]

While the church came together as a whole, smaller groups were also anticipated by Jesus Himself as He gave instructions to His apostles in prayer:

> *"Where two or three are gathered together in my name, there am I in the midst of them."*[32]

Companions in prayer come ready-made in families that have daily devotionals. Extensions of the nuclear family to include those otherwise alone can create a special prayer group. The elders and, at times, the deacons and the minister(s) also form an essential association in prayer. Youth groups, moreover, may be clustered for prayer.

At times, men and women may be separated into distinct prayer groups to allow everyone to pray aloud without usurping authority.

The specific structure of the prayer groups is much less important than the existence of a systematic effort to assure that supplications, prayers, intercessions, and giving of thanks be made for all men,"[33] beginning with the household of faith.

As prayer teams begin to form, the elders will need assurance that there is no violation of scriptural injunctions. One immediate threat to mutual sharing of confession is the risk of self-disclosure. Can a companion in prayer be trusted to maintain confidentiality? Will the person feel inadequate to cope with certain problems, and then, turn to another Christian for "professional help?"

It seems apparent that some problems will need to be referred to another faithful Christian. But this should be the ultimate exception. **For prayer power is available to every child of God.**[34] And it can be practiced by every saint who has been taught to pray.[35]

Besides violation of confidentiality, the worst possible condition is the establishment of a hierarchy. That is, when companions in prayer "cannot" solve problems through mutual confession and prayer,[36] the "senior partner" is advised to "confess" the "junior partner's" sin to the preacher or to the elders. Such a practice can be highly destructive because of loss of confidentiality. The "senior" becomes little more than a tale-bearer, or a gossip. Moreover, the connotation of James 5:16 is that a person must confess his own sins not "report" those of another.

Current practice is often equally bad, for a Christian will hear a confession of sin and merely pass it on. This is a clear violation of scripture. Having spent the past 17 years in my prayer closet offering intercession for others who are truly hurting, it is my firm conviction that a Christian does not have the right to hear a confession of another unless he is willing to pray with and for that person in some private place used as a prayer closet. My experience is always to "weep with those who weep"[37] and always to pray specifically concerning every need without *ever* needing to violate confidentiality.

5. Special Prayer Services

The formation of prayer groups brings a readiness for special services devoted exclusively to prayer. With the elders' approval, perhaps one Sunday evening (or mid-week service) per month could be devoted to prayer. The designation of one Saturday night per month has found favor in some congregations.

When special works are being undertaken, the elders could call the congregation together to pray. For example, when new elders are being ordained,[38] when personal work programs need laborers,[39] when deacons are appointed to special works,[40] when special mission work is being undertaken,[41] when crises arise,[42] when the elders deem it appropriate, let us all pray with one accord.[43]

Could it not be safely concluded that the church that really prays together stays together?

6. Providing Instructions in Prayer Power

"Lord, teach us to pray"[44] caused Jesus to provide

immediate and continuing instruction in prayer power. And so, disciples in the present age should also be taught to pray.

Instructions in prayer power can be provided in a variety of ways.

PRAYER POWER SEMINARS:

Dr. George M. Brown of 7764 West 16 Avenue, Hialeah, Florida, (305) 822-9239, now conducts PRAYER POWER SEMINARS, a major focus of his ministry.

PRAYER POWER CLASSES:

It is suggested that several classes each year be provided for members of the congregation. Perhaps, at the conclusion of a series of lessons, the class could meet in the same time and place for several weeks and engage exclusively in prayer.

PUBLICATIONS ON PRAYER POWER:

Some means may be used to acquaint the congregation with books and articles the elders deem appropriate. If the church has a library, a special section on prayer could be developed. A list of recommended publications might be presented in the bulletin or from the pulpit.

To determine what may best meet the needs of a given congregation, the elders could secure a Gospel Advocate, 20th Century Christian or other respected catalog. Of course, the present author will be pleased to share his conclusions regarding publications currently available.

The Bottom Line

If Christians today -- individually and collectively -- are to change the world, we must become the salt of the earth that has not lost its savor.[45] Only powerful pray-ers have sufficient savor powerful enough to change the world.

The church on its knees will defeat the Devil's most cunning devices. The saint in his prayer closet can change the course of history.

"Vain boasting," you say? Not so, after all, the best theory of aerodynamics demonstrates that the lady bug cannot fly. But, it does! Man can't explain it. And the "best theory" of man is that prayer doesn't work. But it does! For as Jeremiah declared:

> *"Ah, Lord God: behold, Thou hast made the heaven and the earth by thy great power and stretched out arm, and there is nothing too hard for Thee.*[46]

The secret was revealed by the Son of God himself: *"Have faith in God."*[47]

Won't you, fellow Christian, stand in "the gap," and make time to pray?

For as Jesus promised,

> *"If ye have faith as a grain of mustard seed, ye shall say to this mountain; Remove hence to yonder place; and it shall remove; and nothing shall be impossible unto you."*[48]

Won't you begin to sign your name on the next-to-the-last-line, and then on the bottom line write, MOUNTAIN MOVER?

```
    _____
   /        \
  /          \
 |   STOP     |
  \          /
   _____/
```

Chapter X

THAT WE MIGHT ALL BE ONE

"May they be brought to complete unity to let the world know that you have sent me and have loved them even as you have loved me."
-Jesus in John 17:23 (NIV)

Oh, Those Wrecking Crews

Have you ever been involved in a divorce? a church split? the breakup of a business? The effects are so very devastating. Marriage partners have resorted to every tactic from mayhem to murder. Attacks against fellow Christians have ranged from blusters to bombs exploding even as Bible class was being conducted. The chronicles of business breakups lead from conference room to courtroom and even to the cemetery. Indeed, the basic twist to these tragedies is that they happen to those who once pledged their lives and their fortunes to each other. The greater irony, however, is that it grieves God, for He "hates putting away."[1]

Why have such calamities come into our lives? Unity was not important enough! God's method for keeping unity was not used. Like a rusty old plow, prayer power was put aside perhaps in the old barn far away from the house.

Common Prayer

The story is told of a mental institution with every kind of problem known to man. There were 500 patients and only two guards. When someone asked the guards if they weren't afraid of having to guard so many "crazy people," one of them replied, "no, lunatics never organize." In Genesis 4:26, the two hundred and thirty fifth year after creation, we find: the first reference to men coming together to pray (common prayer): "Then began men to call upon the name of the Lord."

Centuries pass before the next reference to common prayer. There we find God's people in bondage that will not end until 430 years will have passed. It is, perhaps, not well understood that their condition has been precipitated by neglect of prayer as a people and ends only *after* they come together as one heart and soul in prayer. In Exodus 3:9, we read the words of Lord God: "The cry of the children of Israel is come up unto me." As the singular reason stated, because of that prayer-cry as a people, the Lord God sent a deliverer -- Moses, under whose leadership they were set free laden with the finest treasures of their masters.

Even less well understood is that the Israelites suffered enslavement a total of 100 additional years even *after* they were in the promised land. Each time they were overrun by their fierce neighbors, the means of securing their deliverance was through common prayer.

The pattern was always the same. The people

☐   **did evil**

☐   **were punished**

☐   **prayed**

☐   **were delivered**

Three generations after Joshua, there arose "a generation that knew not God."[2] Hence, with neglect of common prayer, the Midianites destroyed for seven years. They greatly impoverished God's people, using scorched earth tactics. Then "the children of Israel cried unto the Lord"[3] and were delivered.[4]

God's people did evil and so were mightily oppressed by the Canaanites for 20 years. Then "the children of Israel cried unto the Lord"[5] and "were delivered."[6]

As the people of God neglected worship and did evil, the Lord allowed the Philistines to oppress them for 40 years, until one man and his family -- Manoah -- prayed and brought deliverance.[7]

The Philistines and the Ammonites vexed and oppressed God's chosen for 18 years until, as the record declares: "the children of Israel cried unto the Lord"[8] who once again, rescued them.[9]

In the midst of war with a king gone mad, the record reveals one man whose prayers brought deliverance for the people of God.[10]

Each time, the Lord God sent a deliver in response to prayer. And so, when we read in Hebrews 11, the names in God's "hall of fame," there are certain heroes whose names are mentioned, but their story is not told.

> *"And what shall I say more? for the time would fail me to tell of Gideon, and of Barak, and of Samson, and of Jephthae, and of David and of Samuel, and of the prophets: Who through faith subdued kingdoms, wrought righteousness, obtained promises, stopped the mouths of lions, quenched the violence of fire, escaped the edge of the sword, and out of weakness were made strong, waxed valiant in fight, turned to flight the armies of the aliens. Women received their dead raised to life again...."[11]*

In *every* case, prayer was the *exclusive* means that brought the deliver who performed mighty works to free God's people.

How does it happen? So many times for a nation to fall, and to be delivered through prayer. Surely, God's people ought to have learned something! Yet, it has been aptly stated, "Those who do not remember their history are doomed to repeat it." For as the preacher stated, "There is no remembrance of former things."[12]

Having forgotten their history of dramatic rescues when their communication was fixed in heaven,[13] the Israelites found themselves once again in captivity. Having been reduced to the savagery of eating their own children[14] as food during the final siege of Jerusalem and having experience a 150 mile forced march that included women and children,[15] God's chosen people remained in captivity until one man "wept, mourned, fasted and prayed certain days."[16] Then others would join the prayer cry for freedom and their supplication would be successful.

Even a people not of God -- "heathen" -- changed the mind of the Lord. "I will destroy this people. But when they cried mightily unto the Lord God -- in sackcloth and ashes -- He "repented of the evil He said He would do and did it not."[17]

When Jesus' disciples saw Him in prayer and the results He achieved, they asked: "Lord, teach us to pray."[18] Jesus answered, "When ye (plural of thou) pray..." implied common prayer as did His sermon-on-the-mount description of disciples in worship.

The new established church of Christ *as a body* as well as individuals **"continued steadfastly in prayers."**[19] And so, they grew and had unity.[20]

That's why, when persecutions came and even the apostles were threatened and the flickering flame could be snuffed out, the church came together and prayed:

"Lord behold their threatenings: and grant unto thy servants, that with all boldness they may speak thy word. By stretching forth thine hand to heal; and that signs and wonders may be done by the name of the holy child Jesus. And when they had prayed, the place was shaken where they were assembled together; and they were all filled with the Holy Ghost, and they spake the word of God with boldness."[21]

On virtually every important occasion, the new-born church came together and prayed

☐   When elders were appointed. [22]

☐   When missionary journeys started - and ended. [23]

☐   When benevolent works were undetaken.[24]

☐   When there were church problems and church victories.[25]

Lifting The Veil

Prayer power has not ended. It continues to this day. Dear reader, please refer to Chapter 12, "Present-Day Prayer Power" for confirmation of this point.

The picture is not complete, however, until we lift the veil. Let us turn to Revelation and attest to what John saw when the Lord God gave him a picture of heaven. Indeed, the most frequently developed theme in the book of Revelation is the throne of God, depicted for us 45 different times.

Upon one occasion, before the throne of God, 24 elders are pictured as casting down their crowns before Him and saying:

> *"Worthy art thou, Oh, Lord, to receive glory and honor and power: for thou hast created all things, and for thy pleasure they are and were created."*[26]

Upon the same occasion, we are shown four beasts that give glory and honor and thanks to him that sat on the throne:

> *"Holy, holy, holy, Lord God Almighty, which was, and is, and is to come."*[27]

Shortly thereafter, we learn that the function of the elders and beasts is to carry about *"golden vials full of odors, which are the prayers of the saints."*[28] In addition, John tells of an angel whose function it is to carry a golden censor -- with much incense, *"...that he should offer it with the prayers of all saints upon the golden alter which was before the throne. And the smoke of the incense, which came with the prayers of the saints, ascended up before God out of the angel's hand."*[29]

John relates that he heard the voice of 100,000,000 angels praising God together as one:

> *"Worthy is the lamb that was slain to receive power, and riches, and wisdom, and strength, and honor, and glory, and blessing."*[30]

The prophet also sees a great multitude before the throne -- which no man could number, of all nations, of all people, and of all tongues -- declaring

> *"Salvation to our God, which sitteth upon the throne, and unto the Lamb."*[31]

For before that throne there will be no more death, no more hunger, no more pain, no more thirst, no more night, no more tears.[32] "The Lamb shall feed them and shall lead them into living fountains of waters, *"and God shall wipe away all tears from their eyes."*[33]

What Must We Do?

With so much "putting away," perhaps we should start building monuments to wrecking crews. Or, we must "endeavor to keep the unity of the Spirit in the bond of peace"[34] by using the Lord God's most efficacious means of achieving our aims -- **prayer power.** Then, and only then, will we realize "how good and how pleasant it is to dwell in unity."[35] For perfect peace[36] comes by keeping our conversation fixed in heaven.[37]

Chapter XI

SOME WELL-GUARDED SECRETS

> "...if you look for it as for silver and search for it as for hidden treasure, then you will...find the knowledge of God."
> -Proverbs 2:4, 5 (NIV)

Picture a Dream

The land lay fallow! Nobody had cultivated it in years. In places, the weeds had grown knee high and unsightly brush looked like tightly bunched clusters of small trees. Casual passers-by had no way on knowing of the shattered dream that called for building homes to care for abused/abandoned children. Yet, because hard times had hit with unrelenting force and the original band of believers had become so small in number, it appeared that the goal would not become a reality until "heaven knows when."

One prayer warrior, however, refused to give up on the dream. Consequently, he challenged the congregation, as the prophet Haggai had once done. "Consider your ways."[1] At the first mention of the desire to do this good work, a wonderful Christian couple gave $6,000 to the cause. Later, that same family, Bob and Edna Bishop, would also contribute almost half of their earthly possessions -- $120,000 -- to build the first two homes. Bob Bishop was, at the time, 70 years of age and suffered greatly from heart disease and his wife Edna had cancer removed from 13 places in her body. They would, perhaps, have personal needs they could not meet. Yet, their compassion spoke volumes by the sacrifice they made on behalf of otherwise homeless children.

For some, the story may seem to strain credulity. Yet, not only is it true, it is *not the exception* for the prayer warrior who has learned some well-guarded secrets about prayer power.

Let's Share Some Secrets

Secret #1:

There is a correlation between the physical and the spiritual. Consider, for example, the challenge of Jesus:

> *"Give and it shall be given unto you; good measure, pressed down, and shaken together, and running over...."*[2]

Many believers stop right there and *cannot* finish the sentence. Yet, the correlation is inescapable that Jesus is not speaking exclusively of a spiritual blessing. For He assures you that when you give generously, **"men shall heap into your bosom"**[3] "good measure" that even the casual passer-by can see.

Solomon understood well the intimate connection between the physical and the spiritual when he prayed at the dedication of the temple. He asked the Lord rhetorically

> *"Will God in very deed dwell with men on the earth?"*[4]

Then, while declaring to his maker that even the highest heavens "cannot contain thee,"[5] begged that when there is drought, famine, plagues, or siege "because your people have sinned against you," hear from heaven and forgive and bring an end to these calamities. Then he concluded,

> *"Now, my God, may your eyes be open and your ears attentive to the prayers offered in this place."*[6]

The record declares that the Lord God both understood and accepted the physical-spiritual reciprocity. For His answer came in exact correspondence with the prayer:

> *"When I shut up the heavens so that there is no rain, or command locusts to devour the land or send a plague among my people, if my people, who are called by my name, will humble themselves and pray and seek my face and turn from their wicked ways, then will I hear from heaven and will forgive their sin and will heal their land. Now my eyes will be open and my ears attentive to the prayers offered in this place."*[7]

The method by which the outpouring of blessings comes is through prayer power. A most beautiful correlation appears as a prayer by the apostle John:

> *"Beloved, I wish above all things, that thou mayest prosper and be in health even as your soul prospers."*[8]

Note that good health and financial success are inextricably interwoven with the well-being of one's soul -- implicitly sustained through prayer power. Be apprised of the strength of the prayer wish - ***"above all things."***

The theory has been put to the test on at least one occasion. In a study undertaken at the San Francisco General Medical Center's coronary care unit in 1982 and 1983, Dr. Randolph Byrd divided 393 patients between a group whose health was prayed for by three to seven born-again Christians and a control group that did not receive such prayers. Patients were not told which group they were in. But those who were prayed for had fewer complications during their stay. Dr. John Thomison, editor of the Southern Medical Journal, which published the full study, stated, "Prayer is about as benign a form of treatment as there is."[9]

The Lord God challenged the children of Israel who found themselves in captivity:

> *"For I know the plans I have for you...plans to*
> *prosper you and not harm you, plans to give you*
> *a hope and a future."*[10]

He reveals the secret: "Call upon me and come and pray to me, and I will listen to you."[11]

Secret #2: **"I just can't get answers. It's as if I had not prayed."**

1. **Lack of fervent specificity.** When the tax collector cried, "Lord be merciful to me a sinner,"[12] Jesus commended him. Yet, here was a publican, one unschooled in prayer. Assume that he becomes one of God's born-again beautiful prayer warriors. As such, he will also become increasingly sensitive to specific sins and will want forgiveness for each one. John makes this clear when he writes to the believers:

> *"If we confess our sins, he is faithful and just to*
> *forgive us our sins, and to cleanse us from all*
> *unrighteousness."*[13]

Note that is more than recognition of one's sinful state must recognized. *"Sins"* has now been pluralized.

Not infrequently a fervent cry demands greater specificity. Recall, for example, that Bartameas had pleaded with his entire being for mercy--not once, but twice. Even so, Jesus, asked him to be specific. "What do you want me to do for you"?[14] Surely, our Lord knew what the man wanted, but still inquired in a way that the petitioner asked precisely: "Oh, that I might receive my sight."[15]

2. **Lack of reasons.** "Produce your cause saith the Lord; bring forth strong reasons." Recall, for example, that when Hezekiah begged with fervent specificity his life be extended, he did exactly as the prophet Isaiah received the message from the Lord:

> *"I beseech thee, O Lord, remember how I have walked before thee in truth and with a perfect heart, and have done that which is good in thy sight."*[16]

3. **Lack of thankfulness.** Paul encouraged the Thessalonians "in every thing give thanks."[17] Please note that *"every thing"* is not a compound word. Rather, it requires fervent specificity in giving thanks for each event in our lives. Sometimes, it may even mean expressing gratitude for something bad. For example, during World War II, Corrie Tinn Boom, found herself in a Nazi concentration camp where captors confiscated personal possessions, including even one's Bible. She found a place where her captors would not look - a flea-infested crack in the wall. She thanked God for the fleas.

Fervent specificity in thanksgiving may call forth frequent repetition in response to a single gift. Such was

the case when the Corinthians gave willingly and
liberally to help the impoverished saints in Jerusalem.
Paul repeatedly thanked them in prayer and perhaps in
person:

> *"The administration of this service not only
> supplies the want of the saints, but is abundant
> by many thanks."*[18]

Contrast that with the account of the married couple
celebrating their silver anniversary.

> Wife: "You haven't told me such in a long time that
> you love me."
> Husband: "I told you 25 years ago that I love you;
> and if I ever change my mind, I'll let you know."

Yet, one may counter, "The Lord knows I'm thankful.
Why state the obvious"? Consider, for example, however,
that expression of thanks brings by Jesus himself.
Otherwise, when he cleansed the 10 lepers and only one
came back to articulate his appreciation, Why did he ask:

> *"Were not all ten cleansed? Where are the other
> nine? Was no one found to return and give
> praise to God except this foreigner"?*[19]

Indeed, the pray-er is warned that his petitions may be
hindered unless they are *each one* accompanied by
appreciation:

> *"Be careful for nothing; but in every thing by
> prayer and supplication with thanksgiving let
> your requests be made known unto God."*[20]

David, the man after God's own heart, rose at midnight "...to give thanks for thy righteous judgments."[21] "Seven times a day I give thee thanks...."[22]

4. **Lack of fasting with prayer.** An entire chapter in this book has been devoted to fasting. Yet, the basic essence of that discussion warrants a brief revistation. For many refuse to fast. Yet, Jesus commended fasting. In His Sermon on the Mount, He used the singular and the plural to describe occasions of fasting: "when ye (all of you together) fast" and "when thou fastest."[23]

The spiritual giants fasted. Ezra and other slaves fasted and prayed for the Lord's protection rather than that of an armed guard for a long and perilous journey to freedom.[24] Esther fasted -- and must also have prayed -- to erase the writ of death that would wipe out an entire people, including herself, in all probability.[25] Moses engaged in two 40-day prayer fasts when he was on Mount Sinai to receive the commandments and statutes and to save the lives of all of his own people whom he loved more than he did his own life.[26] David related how fasting enhanced his prayer power: "My clothing was sackcloth: I humbled my soul with fasting: and my prayer returned into my bosom."[27]

Do we not hear someone protest: "But I can't fast." Rather, what is the person without *valid medical reason* not to fast really saying, "I can't fast because I won't fast." Yes, there is something one must give up. David declared, "My knees are weak through fasting and my flesh fails because of fasting." Yet, one must realize the great gain through fasting with prayer. For as Jesus stated, "This kind goes not out but by prayer and fasting."[28]

5. **Prayer must not be self-centered.** When Jesus taught his apostles that the Lord God would grant

"whatsoever" one should ask, He stated that requests should be for the glory of God.[29] Yet, contrast that admonition with the supercilious utterance of the man who intoned: "God bless me, my wife, our two children -- us four and no more." On the other hand, consider the man who was with his best friend in the woods one day when a 2,000 pound bear charged directly toward them. The man bent down to put on his tennis shoes. His friend asked, "Why are you doing that? You can't outrun that bear." To which the man replied, "I know, but I can outrun you."

There is no constraint with the Lord. To the truly generous person the Lord God promises "...to throw open the floodgates of heaven and pour out so much blessing that you will not have room enough for it."[30] Yet, to the selfish persons, He closes the windows of heaven. Can't you realize how much He'd like to bless you. Yet, He can't. You just won't let him. You're too selfish. You measure out your gifts in a spoon and He's using a bucket. Can't you see the mess it would make!

The words of Jesus make this reality quite clear: "With the measure you use, it will be measured to you."[31]

Secret #3: **You get what you pray for.** Hence, be careful in selecting the blessings you seek. Robert Penn Warren in his short story entitled "Blackberry Winter" has his readers meet "Ole Jebb" who tells a young friend, "When I was young, I prayed to the Lord. 'Just give me strength for to endure. And the Lord gave me my strength. But now I am an old man. My wife has died. All of my children are dead. All of my friends are dead. A man just don't know what to pray for and him only human."

King Hezekiah had his supplication answered by having 15 years added to his life. Yet, the record declared that he "...rendered not again according to the benefit done unto him; for his heart was lifted up."[32] Therefore, much evil came upon the people of God because of this.

Let each penitent believer *first* ask for wisdom. "If any of you lack wisdom," James encourages, "let him ask of God...."[33]

For as Solomon realized, "Wisdom is the principal thing; therefore, get wisdom: and with all thy getting get understanding."[34]

Secret #4: **Let the mind of Christ be in you.** Throughout his baptism, He was praying.[35] For 40 days, He fasted.[36] Was it not His *habit* to pray. Upon at least one occasion, He arose before daybreak and went to a solitary place and prayed.[37] At another time, at the end of a long and difficult day, He prayed.[38] At least once, He prayed all night long.[39] At His transfiguration, it was "*as* He prayed" that the fashion of His countenance prayed. At the last supper, His longest recorded prayer presses for unity.[40] In the garden, He prayed first upon His knees,[41] then prostrate upon the ground,[42] and finally in writhing and anguish.[43] During His trials, did He not also for one who would carry on the work after His departure?[44] On the cross, He prayed even for His enemies.[45] As He ascended, He was praying.[46] He ever lives to make intercessions for those who put their trust in Him.[47]

Standing in the Gap

Has not the rampage of sin become so devastating that the Lord God will *soon* release the fire that will destroy the earth and all things in it?[48] Is not the earth filled with violence?[49] Is not every imagination filled with evil, as in the days before the flood?[50] Is the community in which you live, the state, the nation, even the world only a few prayer-ers from destruction? The Lord God once told Ezekiel,

> *"I looked for a man among them who would build up the wall and stand before me in the gap in behalf of the land so I would not have to destroy it, but I found none."*[51]

Soldiers who rush into battle with little training are easily overwhelmed. Let each prayer warrior prepare for doing battle with Satan who goes about "as a roaring lion, seeking whom he may devour."[52]
Listen to the Lord:

> *"For I know the plans I have for you, declares the Lord, plans to prosper you and not to harm you, plans to give you hope and a future."*[53]

Chapter XII

PRESENT-DAY PRAYER POWER

"Blessed is that man that maketh the Lord his trust...."
-Psalm 40:4

"God is Dead"

A person who prayed and could not "feel" the presence of God concluded, "God is dead." And surprisingly, leading theologians began to trumpet that the Lord God does not enter into the affairs of man as he did during "Bible times." Yet, the Lord God has stated, "I change not."[1] Thus, if He ever answered prayer, as has been demonstrated throughout this book, He still answers prayer today.

It is evident that *many* Saints today have failed to pray because they believe that somehow God has changed. But the real problem is within the prayers of the pray-ers.

The traditional "prayer meetings" has become a thing of the past. Efforts to revive it have met with indifference. One congregation, for example, called for all of its 400 members to assemble for an hour of prayer. At first, approximately 50 came. Then, within six months only the elders and the ministers "remembered" to come.

Abandonment of congregational meetings devoted exclusively to prayer time has also witnessed of personal prayer time. In a class of fifty, for example, the teacher discovered that only one other person was spending at least one sweet hour of prayer on a daily basis. Though it was at the end of the day and on a Wednesday evening when the "most faithful" were present, many had not prayed at all that day. In fact, fewer than ten others had spent at least ten minutes in prayer.

Results of a national survey published by the University church of Christ in Denver, Colorado, indicates that one out of every four Christians never personally prays. The resultant conspiracy of silence is broken only on ocassion by the stone-hearted chorus of the first century Laodiceans - "I have need of nothing."[2]

The challenge to "buy gold tried in the fire"[3] given to the Laodiceans carries the same promise today:

> *"To him that overcomes will I grant to sit with me in my throne, even as I also overcame, and am set down with my Father in His throne."*[4]

If you worship in a congregation where truly faithful ones cannot be found, you alone can become the instrument of God's grace by becoming one who can answer "Yes" to the Lord's, "What, could ye not watch with me for one hour?"[5] For Jesus commanded, "Watch and pray, that ye enter not into temptation."[6]

Results That Can Be Seen

The stories you are about to read are true in every detail. In some cases names have been changed to preserve the privacy of persons concerned. Your writer has - over the years - served as an evangelist in several congregations of the church of Christ. Moveover, for 15 years he served as a Christian counsellor and has conducted Prayer Power Seminars spanning 10 years and covering six of these United States.

Congregations Have Been Preserved

At the time of our first association, they were a very small congregation, wrestling with doubts as to whether to shut the doors forever. Their best efforts still left them dependent upon financial support from other churches for their very existence. Then, at the Wednesday evening service following a Prayer Power Seminar, a brother stood before the faithful few and stated, "You heard Dr. Brown challenge us to supplicate and the Lord God would answer in a positive way if we would use the blessing to his glory. We receive around $600 per week in free-will offerings. We need at least $800 to meet our budget. I challenge each of us to pray (supplicate) that we have at least $800 this coming Lord's day."

The collection was $864 that Lord's day in February and increased to over $1,000 per week. During this time, the congregation began to use their blessing to help homeless children in their area and to undertake a mission effort in Haiti.

Several years later, as the nation experienced a significant economic downturn, nearly half of their members had to move when their company either closed or transferred them. And so, the once again feeble flock requested another Prayer Power Seminar. This time their supplication was for souls. One evening, as recipients of their support for homeless children, we received a telephone call that I vividly recall:

"I was supposed to call you about two months ago and tell you that we were going to have to discontinue your support. However, we remembered how you taught us to supplicate. And so, we began to pray for souls. We began to have 50 visitors per service. We now have greater attendance and contribution than ever.

And so, I'm calling you tonight to let you know that we are doubling our contribution to your work on behalf of otherwise homeless children."

In another congregation, the recession had created a crunch of significant size. And so, one Lord's day evening one of the elders advised the flock that was now dwindling in size and in resources. He stated that the elders had concluded that the church could not afford to employ a full-time preacher -- or one on even a part-time basis. Moreover, the preacher's house was being sold to prevent loss of the building of worship itself. The special building project for homeless children would have to be postponed indefinitely. Some partially-paid-for land could not be sold without threatening the loss of the rest of the property -- including the very place of worship itself.

Upon hearing that presentation, this writer asked the elders to be permitted to speak the following Lord's day evening. At that time, the congregation was reminded how the Lord God has rescued his people time and again when they call upon Him -- one thrilling account after another of otherwise imposssible victories were claimed through Prayer Power. Indeed, the boast was made, "The Lord God does his best work when things are the worst. I challenge every one of his precious children to supplicate - supplicate - supplicate."

Within the calendar year, *every one* of these supplications was answered affirmatively: a full-time preacher was hired, the land was sold at a fair price, a new preacher's home was purchased, a special $10,000 contribution was taken for benevolence, and construction on homes for otherwise homeless children was begun.

One congregation noticed a 50 percent increase in the number of souls being saved after special supplications as a people of God. Indeed, as one member expressed, "The church is growing by personal evangelism daily."

Do we not hear him say, "Thou shalt call, and I will answer thee: thou wilt have a desire to the work of thine hands."[7]

Individuals Who Have Been Helped

Having made a special appeal for a work on behalf of homeless children, this writer was advised by the brother who had arranged the speaking engagement:

> *"It doesn't look as though the congregation will be supporting your work (later they would and have continued to this day), but my wife Dorothy and I have already done so. We've made arrangements with our bank to give an amount each month."*

Then he began to cry. He stated that he faced critical surgery within two weeks with only a 50-50 chance of survival and less chance ever to live a normal life again. Whereupon, I invited him to a private place and we supplicated regarding his health. We produced the cause. We brought forth strong reasons -- how he would give for homeless children even though he might not even survive!![8]

His health improved so that the surgery was postponed for two weeks, then a month, then a year. That was more than six years ago. The recovery of that dear brother, one Gerald Schwall, has caused this writer to place his name in the Bible beside Psalm 41:1-3:

> *"Blessed is he that considereth the poor: the Lord will deliver him in time of trouble.*

The Lord will preserve him, and keep him alive;
and he shall be blessed upon the earth: and
thou wilt not deliver him into the will of his
enemies.
The Lord will strengthen him upon the bed of
languishing: thou wilt make all his bed in his
sickness."

He was only six months of age when Diana found him in conditions so horrible few of our readers could easily attend. At six months of age, he faced critical brain surgery with only a slim chance of survival and less chance of ever being close to normal. Though abandoned by his biological parents, one compassionate Christian lady was there in tearful supplication even as little Chris had to scream through the post-operative without anesthetic.

Diana Baglin took little Chris into her own home and has been raising him as her very own. That was six years ago. Thanks to Diana and prayer power, Chris has a wonderful life and the promise of a great future. Last year, Chris claimed every major award in his kindergarten class. Recently, Diana called and told us that, Chris, now in the first grade, had made the honor roll.

Isn't it amazing what prayer power and Christian love will do?

Jeremiah, Chris, and Michael were throw-away kids with no measurable IQ's. They looked so starved and emaciated. Then, a beautiful Christian couple took them into their own home. And after two years in the home of George and Alicia Barrett, the IQ's of the three brothers were measured again. This time, Jeremiah, the eldest, and Michael, the youngest, were tested as normal. But Chris, the middle child, was tested as gifted. The boys have since been adopted by the Barretts and are growing into handsome, young Christian gentlemen. Isn't it truly amazing what prayer power, combined with Christian compassion, will do?

Call him Jabez. His wife's father had just passed away; and as they prepared for the funeral in a distant state from Jabez' home, the telephone company called demanding payment for the business phone - three months overdue. Other debts has been mounting for some time also three month's overdue - debts he saw no way of being able to pay. And so, he prayed to the Lord, "help me to pay my bills -- my just debts, and I will give my time to you." And the Lord God not only "Paid the debts;" for Jabez said, "I didn't do anything to earn it."

As the Lord blessed Jabez, he was faithful to his promise. As Jabez gave his time to the Lord, the Lord gave him a business whereby Jabez "made $1,000,000 without working for it."

His advice to me was that "we should ask the Lord for material blessings, if we will use whatever we have for the Lord. The Lord has buckets full of money if we'll use it for him."

Not only has Jabez had his own time, but he has personally provided full support for missionaries. He has helped Christian schools beyond measure. He has spearheaded a drive to bring low-cost housing for hundreds of the needy elderly of his community. Because he is not a boastful person, who knows how many countless others he has helped.

The name Jabez was not chosen by accident. For we read of his prayer in I Chronicles: "Oh, that Thou wouldst enlarge my coast and that thine hand might be with me and that Thou wouldst keep me from evil, and that it may not grieve me!"[9]

Having recently met with the man we have called Jabez, this writer has been requested by "Jabez" to reveal his name: Robert Forcum.[10] He has further encouraged:

> *"My soul shall make her boast in the Lord: the humble shall hear thereof, and be glad. Oh magnify the Lord with me, and let us exalt his name together."*[11]
> *"In God we boast all the day long, and praise thy name for ever."*[12]

Call her Lucille, a woman who brought a burden on her heart to the pulpit one Lord's day morning. It was time for the worship. But she had to squeeze in her urgent request. "My husband is out on the golf course this morning. Oh, how I wish he were here, worshipping with us." Tears welled unshamedly in her eyes as she spoke. Because time was so precious, the answer given by this writer/speaker was in a single word, "Supplicate." The look we exchanged disclosed of a great guilt. In her face, was a search for hope turned to a look of bewilderment. Then, she went quickly back to her seat. And we didn't speak again for another six months when once again services were about to begin. And this time, too, everything would have to wait until she had shared her message with me. She told me something never to be forgotten:

> *"You remember the last time we spoke? Well, when you told me to supplicate, I was so angry I could have slapped your face. I had already prayed that my husband would become a Christian. But I had given up. For awhile I was so upset I couldn't pray. Then, I did. And I didn't give up until I got the answer I sought."*

"Don't look now but (she pointed through her body) there he sits. He's a Christian now. I just wanted to thank you and to tell you that prayer power really works."

One cannot but hear echoes of the heart of Hannah who would not let go until she had the answer she sought.[13]

Refer to him as Abe. He had been promised the second highest position in the corporate ladder. Yet, within 90 days of the date he accepted the "appointment," he was cruelly cast down. He was required to spend 40 days in a back room with nothing to do. He didn't know what he had done wrong, but there he was, in disgrace, with only a total of three "friends" to come by and try his patience.

Even as Abe prayed to the Lord to restore his good name, he began another kind of prayer ministry on behalf of others that continues to this day. During the 15 years of this service, Abe has seen prayer power beyond one's ability to utter.[14] Consider, for example, the following.

Not one marriage ended in divorce when the couple had come for counselling and prayer. In one case, the divorce papers had been prepared and the court date was set. In another instance, the woman had been a prostitute; and the man, a mafia-connected figure. In still another, there had been an attempted murder. Others, with varying degrees of difficulty were all saved without exception, because marriage was God's idea[15] and prayer power is God's way of preserving it.[16] What psychiatrist without prayer power can make such a claim?

Three-time losers also found release from their tortured anguish. One, for example, had exposed himself "thousands of times." Subsequently, he had seen so many psychiatrists he couldn't remember and had been placed in a mental institution on three occasions. But through prayer power, even as police closed in on the "flasher," he voluntarily turned himself in and told the police they didn't have to worry about him anymore. And they haven't. He's been restored to his wife and family - completely cured.

Another man found himself strapped down for 72 hours in a mental hospital. He had been labeled as "dangerous to himself and others." Psychiatrists wanted this three-time loser put away for good, but the judge released him provisionally to the counsel of Abe. Six months later, Abe was able to assure the judge that there would be no more trouble, for the man who lost every job within two weeks of initial employment was now a "teddy bear" and was able to establish an excellent work record.

A woman was ready to have herself committed to a mental ward. She couldn't hold a job. After a period of prayer therapy, she called Abe one day to declare her cure "like a miracle." She spoke of the harmony in her home, the outstanding ratings and promotion she had received, and the perfect peace she now enjoyed in the Lord.[17]

The Lord God has used Abe's prayers as a vital means of showing His unlimited and unfailing powers on behalf of others. And as Abe has grown in his giving, the Lord has caused men "to heap into his bosom."[18] For he now has his good name restored, having been named as the only person of his professional category to receive his corporation's very highest honor. The honor came just three months after the institution's president swore that he would not bestow such an honor upon anyone - especially Abe. But the same prayer power that changed a Pharoah's mind was still at work as Abe was honored in the presence of all as the only teaching faculty member at Miami-Dade Community College ever to be promoted - during its 31-year history - to the rank of Distinguished Service Professor.

The name Abe has been borrowed from the Biblical character Abraham, referred to as "the friend of God,"[19] and "the father of the faithful."[20]

It is the desire of the author of Prayer Power to use all of the proceeds from this book as well as other contributions toward helping otherwise homeless children, a work that was begun in 1982.

At the first public mention of the effort to help homeless children, an elderly Christian couple gave $6,000. During that first year, 1982, we spent $6,000 for the helpless little ones and still had $6,000 in the bank. That same Christian couple, Bob and Edna Bishop, would later contribute $120,000 that enabled us to build our first two homes -- not dormitories!

It is anticipated that by the end of 1991, there will be 20 Christian couples in the South Florida area will be caring for over 50 otherwise homeless children. Five of those homes are on a 2.4 acre site allocated by the church of Christ at 7700 West 20 Avenue, Hialeah, Florida.

The property is located alongside the Palmetto Expressway, the most heavily traveled road in the county. Indeed, the light does shine upon this good work before the world that "others may see your good works and glorify your Father which is in heaven."[21]

With the family under assault from all quarters, the need is ever increasing. Last year, in Dade County, Florida, alone there were 11,000 cases of abuse of children -- 10,000 of them sexual according to Tim Lewis, Assistant Director of Independent Living, for Health and Rehabilitative Services in Dade County. These, of course, are only the *reported* cases.

One Christian couple has three natural children but has chose to reserve 25 percent of whatever they leave in this world to otherwise homeless children through Christian Homes for Children, Inc., 7764 West 16 Avenue, Hialeah, Florida 33014. Others are making equally impressible commitments to this good work.

Prayer Power Seminars Available

For the past 10 years, this writer has conducted Prayer

Power Seminars in churches of Christ in six different states. He has received, as Mark Twain once stated, "some of the kindest words ever vouched upon any wandering alien on this planet, I think." Because of the success of the Prayer Power Seminars, an effort is being made to share in print as well as from pulpit a message of hope -- a message that reveals more fully how each of God's born-again beautiful[22] can realize the full potential in his/her own life of prayer power: the greatest force in the world.

Chapter XIII

ON EAGLE'S WINGS

"We live in an ascending scale when we live happily, one
thing leading to another in an endless series."
-Robert Louis Stevenson

Mounting Up!

Taking her eaglet from the nest, the mother eagle
places her offspring on her back between her wings. She
spreads her wings and soars high into the sky. Then, she
tilts her wings and the eaglet begins its fall toward the
craggy rocks below. The eaglet screams so very loudly! It
tries to fly, but it "can't." Just when the eaglet's heart is
about to burst from fear of splattering on the rapidly
approaching rocks below, the mother eagle swoops below
the eaglet and bears it safely up into the sky again -- and
repeats the experience until the screaming *eaglet* learns
to fly on its own eagle's wings. Isn't this the promise
made by the psalmist:

> *"They mount up to the heaven, they go down
> again to the depths: their soul is melted because
> of trouble. They reel to and fro, and stagger, like
> a drunken man, and are at their wits end. Then
> they cry unto the Lord in their trouble, and he
> bringeth them out of their distress."*[1]

Isn't this the picture painted by the prophet Isaiah:

> *"They that wait upon the Lord shall renew their
> strength; they shall mount up with wings as*

eagles; they shall run, and not be weary; and they shall walk, and not faint."[2]

Rejoicing In Prayer

At that sorrowful scene at the Last Supper, Jesus stated: *"These things have I spoken unto you, that my joy may remain in you, and that your joy might be full."*[3] The psalmist David would describe that joy as "everlasting"[4] and Simon Peter would feel so full that words would be inadequate to describe it.[5]

You have just received the offer of a lifetime. A friend of yours has promised you a new home that will be just wonderful. Yet, upon arrival, you find people already living there who have no plans to move. Then, too, you find the occupants in deep poverty. Hence, you move on to "greener pastures." Twenty years will pass before you are to realize the fulfillment of the promise by your friend. Even then, you have had to beg him for mercy. Then, when he finally does, your joy is indeed "unspeakable." As you have prayed (and fasted?) for three days and nights, you plead for him to spare your son's life -- the one you've even named "laughter" (Isaac). Then he shows you a lamb caught in the brush for the blood offering instead of your son's. As you see the "lamb of God," you look 2,000 down the pages of history and see Jesus Christ -- the true sacrificial lamb -- who states, *"Abraham rejoiced to see my day. He saw it and was glad."*[6] That rejoicing resulted from powerful praying.

Picture this, mountains rising sharply to the left and to the right and a vengeful enemy armed to the teeth closing from behind. The terrified family flees in the only direction it can go until it comes to an impassable body of water. Such was the plight of the newly freed Israelites as their former slave masters chased them to the shore of the Red Sea. They were only a prayer from annihilation. Then when Moses raised the rod of prayer and asked the Lord for deliverance, the sea opened, they passed safely across, and the enemy drowned as the walls of water collapsed, they exulted in song:

> *"Who is like unto thee, O Lord, among the gods? Who is like thee, glorious in holiness, fearful in praises, doing wonders?"*[7]

In response to victory claimed through prayer power, Miriam also led the women in a joyous chorus:

> *"Sing ye to the Lord, for he hath triumphed gloriously; the horse and his rider hath he thrown into the sea."*[8]

She wanted a child so very badly. To her, it was a curse not to be able to get pregnant. So, she risked being charged with being drunk as she mumbled her prayer cry. Yet, she would not accept denial. For the birth of a son, she would not even keep in her own home. She would give him to the Lord. Then, when Hannah gave birth to Samuel, she continued her prayer -- now in ecstatic utterance:

> *"My heart rejoices in the Lord; in the Lord my horn is lifted high. My mouth boasts over my enemies, for I delight in your deliverance. There is no one holy like the Lord; there is no one beside you; there is no Rock like our God. Do not talk so proudly or let your mouth speak such arrogance, for the Lord is a God who knows, and by him deeds are weighed. The bows of the warriors are broken, but those who stumbled are*

armed with strength. Those who were full hire themselves out for food, but those who were hungry hunger no more. She who was barren has borne seven children, but she who has had many sons pines away. The Lord brings death and makes alive; he brings down to the grave and raises up. The Lord sends poverty and wealth; he humbles and he exalts. He raises the poor from the dust and lifts the needy from the ash heap; he seats them with princes and has them inherit a throne of honor. For the foundations of the earth are the Lord's; upon them he has set the world. He will guard the feet of his saints, but the wicked will be silenced in darkness. It is not by strength that one prevails; those who oppose the Lord will be shattered. He will thunder against them from heaven; the Lord will judge the ends of the earth. He will give strength to his king and exalt the horn of his anointed."[9]

Suppose you had just learned of a bribe that would provide the means for extermination of your entire family. What would you do? Would you flee before someone discovered that you were a member of that family also? One woman decided to risk her own life to save her loved ones. She would test the power of fasting (and prayer?) and in so doing would change the course of history. To this day Queen Esther's "family," Jewish people throughout the world, have a very special celebration of that prayer-fast deliverance: Purim, or the bribe. They set aside the fourteenth and the fifteenth days of Adar[10] that they *"...should make them days of feasting and joy, and of sending portions one to another, and gifts to the poor!"*[11]

You have prayerfully yearned for years to have a place of worship where you live. You direct a group in laying the foundation and there is such a loud noise that people at a distance cannot tell whether there is laughing or crying. Actually, according to the record, it is both -- laughing and crying. Yet, must not the tears also be of joy? Study the story occasioned by Ezra's prayers and fasting for that great day in Jerusalem when the people beheld the answer of the Lord God to that prayer warrior's petitions and see that here was joy beyond words.[12]

Your boss likes you so much that the other chief assistants are so jealous of you that they just can't stand it. So, they plot against you. They would like to charge you with incompetence, but your work is superior to theirs. They also look for corruption, but you have been thoroughly honest and morally pure. So, they finally settle upon charging you with disloyalty. You are actually very loyal to your boss -- even more so than the perpetrators of the plot against you. Yet, they go ahead anyway. You see, they have discovered a secret about you. You are a prayer warrior. Thus, the conspirators have secured the signature of your boss that one must petition from him alone - not even God - during a 30-day period. The penalty is death. What are you to do? Give up prayer for 30 days? After all, it's only a short time. Surely, God will understand! Yet, you decide that this would be disloyalty to the "boss of bosses." You will not give up praying. Hence, though your boss suffers a broken heart and prays for you all night long, he follows through with his order and you are suddenly alone in a large pit among hungry lions. Still, they do not attack -- not one even opens his mouth. In the early hours the next day, your boss looks down into the pit and not seeing well cries out for you. Upon hearing your hearty reply, he is "exceeding glad" and orders your perpetrators put in your place. This is the story of the prayer warrior, Daniel, whose life the Lord God spared.

It was a chance in a lifetime to serve at the altar of God - to pray for all the people. It was in only a fleeting moment, perhaps, that he offered one personal, private prayer. Then, in response to Zacharias' prayer for a son, the angel promised *"...thou shalt have joy and gladness, and many shall rejoice at his birth."*[13] Subsequently, when John the Baptist was born, Zacharias was filled with the Holy Ghost and prophesied in a prayer:

> *"Praise be to the Lord, the God of Israel, because he has come and has redeemed his people...to shine on those living in darkness and in the shadow of death, to guide our feet into the path of peace."*[14]

Despite her having been pregnant and despite the length of the journey, she would walk to see her friend who was now in her sixth month. Upon arrival, she would call her friend by name and cause the woman's child to leap in her womb. Whereupon, Elizabeth exclaimed in a loud voice:

> *"Blessed are you among women, and blessed is the child you will bear. But why am I so favored, that the mother of my Lord should come to me"?*
> *"Blessed is she who has believed in what the Lord has said to her will be accomplished."*[15]

We have already noticed that prayer precipitated the pregnancy of Elizabeth. Let us also realize that prayerful submission sent Mary to this wondrous moment. For when the angel announced to Mary that she would be with child of the Holy Ghost, she spoke without hesitation her prayerful, "Amen":

> *"I am the Lord's servant. May it be as you have said."*[16]

Upon hearing Elizabeth's Holy Spirit inspired prophecy, Mary burst forth with her own magnificat:

> *"My soul glorifies the Lord and my spirit rejoices in God my Savior, for he has been mindful of the humble state of his servant. From now on all generations will call me blessed, for the Mighty One has done great things for me -- holy is his name. His mercy extends to those who fear him, from generation to generation. He has performed mighty deeds with his arm; he has scattered those who are proud in their inmost thoughts. He has brought down rulers from their thrones but has lifted up the humble. He has filled the hungry with good things but has sent the rich away empty. He has helped his servant Israel, remembering to be merciful to Abraham and his descendants forever, even as he said to our fathers."*[17]

He had sent them forth to do a good work. Yet, they were to take nothing with them -- no money or even shoes. They had no certain place to sleep. Yet, when they returned and told him the wonderful news of their success, He became "full of joy through the Holy Ghost," and said:

> *"I praise you, Father, Lord of heaven and earth,*

because you have hidden these things from the wise and learned, and revealed them to little children. Yes, Father, for this was your good pleasure."[18]

Part the veil of heaven and view the throne of God where the hallelujah chorus sings.[19] Angels go about with golden sensors spreading the incense of heaven - the prayers of saints.[20] Oh, what joy to join the heavenly host to sing the new song.

Spreading Your Wings

Once the eaglet learns to fly, it no longer needs to screech in terror. Yet, today we hear full-grown eagles (Christians) screaming every time responsibility is thrust upon them. "No! No! I can't visit the sick." "No! No! I can't help a homeless child or a widow." "People in prison -- that's not for me"! "The hungry -- the homeless -- they're all riff-raff, anyway." And one day these eaglets who have been denied the pleasure of selfless giving will also be denied eternal joys with the Lord.[21] Forever they will scream in external torment -- day and night -- along with those who never knew they had wings in the first place.[22]

If you wish to enter into the joy of the Lord God -- to have unspeakable joy eternally, you need to be truly in His family -- born again of water and spirit.[23] He promises to make all things new.[24] Your conversion will cause even the angels in heaven to rejoice.[25]

"The wilderness and the solitary place shall be glad for them; and the desert shall rejoice, and blossom as the rose. It shall blossom abundantly, and rejoice even with joy and

singing: the glory of Lebanon shall be given unto it, the excellency of Carmel and Sharon, they shall see the glory of the Lord, and the excellency of our God. Strengthen ye the weak hands, and confirm the feeble knees. Say to them that are of a fearful heart, Be strong, fear not: behold, your God will come with vengeance, even God with a recompense; he will come and save you. Then the eyes of the blind shall be opened, and the ears of the deaf shall be unstopped. Then shall the lame man leap as an hart, and the tongue of the dumb sing: for in the wilderness shall waters break out, and streams in the desert. And the parched ground shall become a pool, and the thirsty land springs of water: in the habitation of dragons, where each lay, shall be grass with reeds and rushes. And an highway shall be there, and a way, and it shall be called the way of holiness; the unclean shall not pass over it; but it shall be for those: the wayfaring men, though fools, shall not err therein. No lion shall be there, nor any ravenous beast shall go up thereon, it shall not be found there; but the redeemed shall walk there: And the ransom of the Lord shall return, and come to Zion with songs and everlasting joy upon their heads: they shall obtain joy and gladness, and sorrow and sighing shall flee away."[26]

Thus, both now and forever more you will through prayer power realize the ultimate joy - to spread your own wings and soar to the very throne of God. Amen!

Scripture Endnotes

WARNING

[1] Hebrews 4:16

[2] Timothy 2:8

PRAYER POWER REALLY WORKS-- CHAPTER I

[1] Walter B. Knight
Knight's Master
Book of New
Illustrations, Grand
Rapids, Michigan
William B. Eerdman's
Publishing Co., 1958
p. 485

[2] Ibid

[3] Ibid

[4] "Nine out of 10
Americans Pray," a
poll by George Gallop, Jr.
and Jim Castelli, Los Angles
Times Syndicate, reported in
The Miami Herald, Friday
May 19, 1989, p.45

[5] Genesis (NIV) 32:7

[6] Genesis (NIV) 27:40

[7] Genesis (NIV) 32:11

[8] Genesis (NIV) 33:4

[9] Genesis 32:24

[10] Genesis 32:28

[11] Exodus 8:8

[12] Exodus 8:29

[13] Exodus 9:28

[14] Exodus 10:17

[15] Exodus 8:12-14

[16] Exodus 8:31

[17] Exodus 9:33

[18] Exodus 10:18-19

[19] Exodus 10:28

[20] Exodus 11:6 (NIV)

[21] I Samuel 1:1-11

[22] Esther

[23] Ezra 8:21

[24] Ezra 8:21-23, 31

[25] II Kings 19, 20

[26] II Kings 6:16-18

[27] The Pulpit Commentary
editors H. D. M. Spencer
& Joesph S. Exell. Grand
Rapids, Michigan: Jim B.
Eerdman's Publishing Co.
Volume 16, p. 4.

[28] Luke 1:19-20

[29] Luke 1:14

[30] Matthew 11:11

[31] Acts 12:1-15

[32] Acts 2:38

[33] Galatians 5:16

[34] Galatians 5:22-23

[35] Philippians 3:20

[36] Galatians 6:10

[37] Matthew 5:43-48

[38] Romans 12:20

[39] Malachi 3:10

[40] Matthew 23:23

[41] Luke 6:38

[42] John 15:1-10

[43] Matthew 9:37

[44] Matthew 9:38

[45] Ben Johnson Volpone
1605, 5-12

[46] II Peter 1:4

[47] Psalm 2:8

[48] Psalm 18:43

[49] "Prayer May Help
Medical Study Finds
" The Miami Herald
January 23, 1989, p. 12A.

PRAYER POWER UNLIMITED-- CHAPTER II

1 Genesis 18:14

[2] Genesis 18:10

[3] Genesis 18:11, 12, 14;
Ephesians 3:20

[4] Jeremiah 32:26

[5] Jeremiah 32:17

[6] Jeremiah 32:17

[7] For demonstration see
succeeding chapters.

[8] Hebrews 12:1

[9] Romans 12:12

[10] I Timothy 2:8

[11] John 14:13

[12] John 14:14

[13] John 15:7

[14] John 15:16

[15] John 16:23

[16] John 16:24

[17] John 17:24

[18] John 16:31

[19] Matthew 26:30 &
Mark 14:26

[20] I John 5:13-15

[21] I John 5:13-15

[22] John 14:3
Ibid 15:16
Ibid 16:23

[23] John 14:14

[24] I Samuel 14:6

[25] Isaiah 62:6

[26] Isaiah 59:1

[27] II Chronicles 7:14, 15

[28] I Kings 8:37

[29] I Kings 17-18

[30] James 5:17,18

[31] Joel 1:15

[32] Joel 2:13

[33] Joel 1:14

[34] Ezekiel 5:12

[35] Lamentations 3:7, 22, 55, 57

[36] Matthew 7:7

[37] Isaiah 45:5

[38] Isaiah 45:11

[39] Ephesians 5:25-27

[40] Ephesians 3:9

[41] Ephesians 3:20

[42] Acts 2:47

[43] Acts 5:14

[44] Acts 6:7

[45] Acts 2:42

[46] Ephesians 3:8

[47] Revelation 22:1

[48] Philippians 4:6

[49] Alfred Lord Tennyson
"The Passing of Arthur"
Idylls of the King (1869)

[50] Mark 11:24

A HOUSE OF PRAYER--   CHAPTER III

[1] The Washington Post
December 3, 1977, p. 1

[2] Ecclesiastes 1:11

[3] II Peter 1:13

[4] Revelation 20:12

[5] Matthew 12:36

[6] Mark 9:43

[7] Revelation 5:8

[8] Matthew 12:37

[9] I John 3:1

[10] Luke 11:1

[11] Matthew 6:6

[12] John 2:13-16

[13] John 4:24

[14] John 2:19

[15] John 2:21

[16] Matthew 21:9

[17] Matthew 21:10-13

[18] John 2:19, 21

[19] John 3:5

[20] I Corinthians 3:16

[21] I Timothy 3:15

[22] Colossians 4:12

[23] Deuteronomy 10:21

[24] Psalm 8:1

[25] Matthew 6:9
Luke 1:2

[26] Revelation 7:12

[27] Isaiah 6:5

[28] Psalm 51:10

29 Matthew 6:12
30 Romans 3:19
31 Romans 3:23
32 I John 1:8, 10
33 I John 1:9
34 Lamentations 3:22
35 Matthew 10:32, 33
36 Proverbs 27:5
37 Psalm 103:2
38 Psalm 100:4
39 Ephesians 5:20
40 Hebrews 13:15
41 Ephesians 6:11, 18
42 James 5:16
43 Matthew 6:6
44 Luke 18:9-14
45 Philippians 3:20
46 Colossians 4:12
47 Hebrews 4:14
48 Luke 18:11, 12

49 Hebrews 5:7
50 Mark 10:46-52
51 I Samuel 1:27
52 I Samuel 1:11
53 James 5:17
54 James 5:18
55 Psalm 119:164
56 I John 1:8-10
57 I Thessalonians 5:18
58 Philippians 4:6, 7
59 Colossians 4:12
60 Romans 12:12
61 Luke 11:24-26
62 II Peter 2:22
63 Matthew 23:37, 38
64 Matthew 23:14
65 Matthew 26:41
66 Luke 22:46
67 I Peter 3:12
68 Luke 22:46

PRAYER POWER TO CHANGE GOD'S MIND-- CHAPTER IV

1 Malachi 3:6
2 Matthew 25:36
3 Acts 2:38
4 II Peter 1:4
5 II Peter 1:1
6 Jeremiah 33:3
7 Matthew 7:7
8 Genesis 18:20
9 Genesis 18:26
10 Genesis 18:27
11 Genesis 18:21
12 Jonah 3:3
13 Jonah 1:2; 3:4
14 Jonah 3:8
15 Jonah 3:10
16 Nahum 1:1; 3:1, 15
17 Exodus 2:23
18 Exodus 32:10
19 Exodus 32:11-14
20 Psalm 106:23
21 II Kings 20:1
22 II Kings 20:2, 3
23 II Kings 20: 4, 5, 6

24 II Kings 20:7
25 James 5:14, 15
26 Matthew 5:45
27 Job 28:25, 26
28 Genesis 6:5, 13
29 Genesis 7:11, 12
30 I Peter 3:21
31 Leviticus 26:4
   Deuteronomy 11:13-15
32 Leviticus 26:3
33 I Kings 17:1
   James 5:17
34 I Kings 16:30
35 I Kings 18-19
36 Deuteronomy 11:17
37 II Chronicles 7:14
38 I Kings 18:45
39 Luke 11:1-13
40 Luke 18:1-5
41 Luke 18:6-8
42 Luke 18:9-14
43 Luke 13:1-3
44 Luke 11:13

PRAYER POWER THROUGH THE AGES--   CHAPTER V

[1] Haggai 2:7
[2] John 1:14
[3] Colossians 1:26
[4] Genesis 1:26
[5] John 1:1
[6] John 17:22
[7] Genesis 1:26
[8] Philippians 3:20
[9] Genesis 4:26
[10] Herbert Lockyer, All
   the Prayers of the Bible
   (Grand Rapids, Michigan
   Zonderban Publishing
   Company (1976), p. 18
[11] Genesis 3:9-13
[12] Genesis 3:22, 23
[13] Genesis 3:15
[14] I John 3:8
[15] Genesis 6:5-8, 19
[16] Genesis 8:20
[17] Genesis 12:8
[18] Hebrews 13: 10
[19] Isaiah 41:1
   James 2:23
[20] Genesis 18:23-33
[21] Genesis 15:2
[22] Genesis 12:2, 3;
   18:18; 22:18
[23] Matthew 1:24
[24] I Corinthians 12:13
[25] Jeremiah 32:17
[26] Hebrews 11:17-19
[27] Genesis 22:2
[28] John 8:56
[29] Genesis 22:13
[30] John 1:29
[31] Exodus 33:11
[32] Deuteronomy 18:18, 19
[33] John 4:25, 26
[34] John 17:8
[35] Exodus 3:14
[36] Revelation 1:8

[37] John 8:58
[38] Hebrews 13:8
[39] Philippians 2:10, 11
[40] Exodus 14:13-31
[41] Exodus 17:8-16
[42] Exodus 17:6
[43] Psalm 78:16
[44] I Corinthians 10:4
[45] Romans 6:10
[46] Exodus 32:31, 32
[47] John 3:16
[48] Deuteronomy 9:18, 20
   25-29
[49] Exodus 34:29
[50] Luke 9:29
[51] Numbers 27:16
[52] John 16:13
[53] Matthew 16:18
[54] Jude 3
[55] Deuteronomy 34:10
[56] Joshua 10:13
[57] Matthew 27:45, 51-53
[58] Judges 3:9
[59] Judges 3:15
[60] Judges 4:3,4
[61] Judges 6:7, 11
[62] Judges 10:10; 11:1
[63] Luke 2:25, 36-38
[64] Ephesians 2:10-22
[65] I Samuel 1:10
[66] I Samuel 1:11
[67] I Samuel 1:17
[68] I Samuel 2:10
   Psalm 2:1-9
[69] I Samuel 8:7
[70] Matthew 27:45, 51-53
[71] John 5:23, 38-47
[72] Ruth 4:14
[73] Ruth 1:20
[74] Ruth 4:17
[75] Matthew 1:1-25
   Luke 3:23-38

76 I Samuel 12:23, 23
77 I Samuel 10:1-13
78 I Samuel 14:35-37
79 I Samuel 17:45
80 Psalm 2:7
81 John 3:16
82 Psalm 16:10
83 Acts 13:37
84 Psalm 22:1
85 Matthew 27:46
86 Matthew 27:35
87 Psalm 31:5
88 Luke 23:46
89 I Kings 3:5-16; 9:2-9
90 Song of Solomon
91 John 2:12-17
92 John 2:12-17
93 Matthew 21:13
   I Corinthians 3:16-18
94 I Kings 14:1
95 I Kings 18:41-44
96 I Kings 17:20, 21
   II Kings 5:18-37
97 John 2:1-11
98 John 6:15-21
99 John 11:1-46
100 John 19:17-21:25
   Acts 2:1-47
101 Daniel 2:44, 45
102 Matthew 16:16-18
103 John 1:23
104 Matthew 3:2

105 See: **THE PRAYER POWER OF JESUS**
106 Matthew 16:18
107 Acts 1:11-14
108 Romans 3:23
109 Acts 2:38
110 Acts 22:16
111 Acts 2:36-47
112 Acts 2:42
113 Ephesians 3:9, 10
114 Ephesains 3:14-21
115 Acts 4:24
116 Acts 3:1-4, 33
117 Acts 12:5
118 Acts 12:3-19
119 Acts 17:25, 26
120 Acts 7:60
121 Acts 7:56
   Romans 9:3
122 Romans 9:3
123 I Corinthians 1:23
124 II Peter 3:9
125 Acts 6:1-4
126 Acts 10:4
127 Acts 9:9, 11
128 Acs 22:17
129 I John 2:1
130 Hebrews 7:25
131 Acts 13:1-3
132 Acts 14:23
133 Acts 20:36, 27

THE PRAYER POWER OF JESUS-- CHAPTER VI

1 Isaiah 59:8, 9
2 I Corinthians 3:19
3 Hebrews 5:5
4 Hebrews 5:7
5 Luke 22:42
6 Luke 1:8-10
7 Luke 1:13
8 Luke 1:13
9 John 1:29
10 Luke 2:10

11 Luke 2:13, 14
12 Luke 2:25-32
13 Luke 2:37, 38
14 Luke 2:52
15 Luke 1:13
16 Luke 3:21
17 Luke 3:22
18 Luke 24:50, 51
19 Acts 7:55, 56
20 Acts 7:60

21 Hebrews 7:25
22 Mark 1:35
23 Luke 5:15
24 Luke 5:12-16
25 Luke 6:1-12
26 Matthew 14:19
   Mark 6:41
   Luke 9:16
   John 6:11
27 Luke 9:16
28 John 6:15
29 Matthew 14:23
30 I John 2:15-17
31 Mark 8:6, 7
32 I Corinthians 10:31
33 I Thessalonians 5:18
34 John 6:66
35 John 6:67
36 Luke 9:18
37 Matthew 16:16, 17
38 Matthew 17: 1, 2
39 Luke 9:29
40 Luke 9:35
41 Luke 10:3
42 Luke 10:21, 22
43 Luke 9:51
44 Luke 10:4
45 Luke 10:17
46 Matthew 17:14-21
47 Luke 11:1
48 Luke 11:2-4
   Matthew 6:9-13
49 Matthew 6:5-7
50 Luke 11:5-8
51 Luke 11:10-13
52 John 11:41-43

53 Jeremiah 32:17
54 Matthew 19:13-15
55 Matthew 18:1-6
56 Luke 18:17
57 John 12:21
58 John 12:23, 24
59 John 12:28
60 John 12:28
61 John 14:13, 14; 15:7
   16; 16:23, 24
62 John 17:1
63 John 17:6, 9
64 John 17:20, 21
65 Matthew 11:28-30
66 Acts 20:7
67 I Corinthians 11:26-28
71 Luke 22:44
72 Luke 22:44
73 Luke 22:52
74 John 18:10, 11
   Matthew 26:56
75 Luke 22:31, 32
76 I Peter 1:7
77 I Peter 4:7
78 Matthew 27:46
79 Luke 23:34
80 John 19:26
81 John 19:27
82 Luke 23:43
83 Luke 23:46
84 Matthew 16:18
85 Hebrews 5:7
86 Hebrews 7:25
87 Luke 22:42

ATTAINING WISDOM IN PRAYER POWER--   CHAPTER VII

1 Proverbs 4:7
2 Isaiah 55:8
3 I Corinthians 1:20-25
4 James 3:17
5 James 1:5
6 Proverbs 2:3-6

7 Acts 8:35-37
8 James 1:6, 7
9 James 5:15
10 Matthews 9:29
11 Luke 7:50
12 Matthew 21:21

[13] James 4:3
[14] Exodus 16:33
[15] Numbers 11:33
[16] Psalm 106:15
[17] II Corinthians 12:9
[18] James 1:2-4
[19] I Corinthians 1:27
[20] II Corinthians 12:9
[21] Genesis 37:7
[22] Genesis 45:8
[23] I Peter 1:16
[24] Matthew 6:33
[25] Jeremiah 33:17
[26] Genesis 32:24-30
[27] Isaiah 65:5
[28] Ezekial 31
[29] II Kings 20:1
[30] II Kings 20:2-6
[31] II Chronicles 32:25
[32] II Chronicles 32:26
[33] Romans 12:11
[34] Hebrews 4:16
[35] I Corinthians 14:15
[36] Romans 10:1
[37] Luke 18:2
[38] Luke 18:7
[39] Luke 18:1
[40] Acts 2:42
[41] Galatians 6:9
[42] Psalm 66:18
[43] Isaiah 59:1, 2
[44] Romans 12:12
[45] Psalm 1:2
[46] Hebrews 12:1
[47] Matthew 12:36
[48] Matthew 6:7
[49] Isaiah 65:1
[50] Isaiah 65:24
[51] James 5:16
[52] Job 14:1
[53] James 1:5
[54] Psalm 103:13, 14

INCREASING PRAYER POWER THROUGH FASTING--

CHAPTER VIII

[1] Matthew 5-7
[2] Matthew 6:16
[3] Matthew 6:17
[4] Matthew 6:2, 5, 17
[5] Mark 2:18, 19
[6] Mark 2:20
[7] Mark 1:12
[8] James 1:2-7
[9] Matthew 3:16, 17
[10] Ephesians 6:12
[11] I Corinthians 9:27
[12] Ephesians 2:2
John 12:31
[13] Deuteronomy 6:13
[14] I John 2:16
[15] Matthew 4:1-11
[16] John 3:6
[17] II Corinthians 10:3
[18] Romans 8:9
[19] Romans 8:13
[20] Esther 4:16
[21] Ezra 7:12
[22] Ezra 8:22, 23
[23] Ezra 8:31
[24] Psalm 35:13
[25] Joel 1:6-12
[26] Joel 1:14
[27] Joel 2:12
[28] II Chronicles 7:13, 14
[29] Leviticus 16:29
Leviticus 23:27
[30] Acts 27:1-9
[31] Psalm 84:7; 33:16
Isaiah 40:31
Psalm 59:17
Hebrews 6:5
[32] Matthew 6:5
[33] II Corinthians 11:18, 30
[34] II Corinthians 11:27
[35] II Corinthians 11:26
[36] Judges 19:1-21, 25

[37] I Kings 18:1-II Kings 2:11
[38] Daniel 6:10
[39] Daniel 9:3
[40] Jonah 3:5
[41] Jonah 3:8
[42] Acts 2:42
[43] Acts 12:5
[44] Acts 13:3
[45] Acts 14:1-9
[46] Acts 14:23
[47] II Corinthians 11:26, 27
[48] Romans 11:6
[49] Ephesians 2:5
[50] Luke 18:9-14
[51] Isaiah 58:3
[52] Isaiah 58:3-5 (NIV)
[53] Isaiah 58:6-7, 10 (NIV)
[54] Isaiah 58:10, 11 (NIV)
[55] Henry Bettenson, ed. Documents of the Christian Church (London: Oxford University Press, 1981), p. 77.
[56] J. B. Lightfoot, The Apostolic Fathers ed. J. R. Harmer (Grand Rapids: Baker Book House, 1976) pp. 35, 36, 97.
[57] Ibid., pp. 123, 126.
[58] Ibid., pp. 138, 139, 143, 150.
[59] Ibid., pp. 168, 170, 177 203, 205.
[60] Bettenson, Documents, p. 28.
[61] Alexander Roberts & James Donaldson, eds., "Fathers of the Third Century," The AnteNicene Fathers, IV translated by S. Thelwall (Grand Rapids: William B. Eerdmans Publishing Co., 1969) pp. 102-115.
[62] John Calvin, Institutes of the Christian Religion, II (Philadelphia The Presbyterian Board of Publication, 1909), pp. 424, 427.
[63] R. D. Chatham, Fasting (South Plainfield, New Jersey: Bridge Publishing Company), pp. 90-92.
[64] Eric N. Rogers, Fasting : The Phenomenon of Self-Denial (Nashville: Thomas Nelson, Inc., Publishers, 1976), pp. 71-73.
[65] Derek Prince, Shaping History Through Prayer and Fasting (Old Tappan, New Jersey Fleming H. Revell Co., 1973) pp. 138, 139.
[66] Prince, Shaping History pp. 141-143.
[67] Isaiah 60:1, 2

PRAYER POWER BATTLE PLAN--   CHAPTER IX

[1] Ephesians 6:14-17
[2] Ephesians 6:11
[3] Ephesians 6:11
[4] I Peter 5:8
[5] II Peter 2:21
[6] Ephesians 6:18
[7] II Corinthians 11:14
[8] Romans 5:8
[9] Ephesians 6:18
[10] John 1:14
[11] I Thessalonians 5:17
[12] Psalm 55:17
[13] Daniel 6:10
[14] Acts 2:15
[15] Acts 10:9
[16] Acts 3:1
[17] Matthew 6:5
[18] Ezekiel 22:30
[19] Ezekiel 22:31
[20] II Peter 1:4
[21] James 5:16-20
[22] Exodus 18:21, 22
[23] Exodus 18:14
[24] Exodus 18:17, 18

25 Exodus 18:24
26 Acts 6:1-7
27 I Corinthians 16:1, 2
28 I Thessalonians 5:17
29 Romans 12:12
30 I Peter 2:2
31 Acts 4:31
32 Matthew 18:20
33 I Timothy 2:1
34 I Peter 2:5, 9
   I John 2:1-5
35 Luke 11:1
   James 1:5

36 James 5:16
37 Romans 12:15
38 Acts 14:23
39 Matthew 9:38
40 Acts 6:6
41 Acts 13:1 -3
42 Acts 12:1-19
43 Acts 4:1-34
44 Luke 11:1
45 Matthew 5:13
46 Jeremiah 32:17
47 Mark 11:22
48 Matthew 17:20

THAT WE MIGHT ALL BE ONE--   CHAPTER X

1 Malachi 2:16
2 Judges 2:10
3 Judges 6:7
4 Judges 6:6-8
5 Judges 4:3
6 Judges 4:5
7 Judges 13:8
8 Judges 10:10
9 Judges 10:6-12:7
10 I Samuel 15
11 Hebrews 11:32-35
12 Ecclesiastes 1:11
13 Philippians 3:20
14 Lamentations 2:20;
   Jeremiah 19:9
15 Jeremiah 52:24-30
16 Nehemiah 1:4
17 Jonah 3:8-10
18 Luke 11:1

19 Acts 2:42
20 Acts 4:32
21 Acts 4:29-31
22 Acts 14:23
23 Acts 13:3
24 Acts 6:4
25 Acts 20:17-36
26 Revelation 4:11
27 Revelation 4:8
28 Revelation 5:8
29 Revelation 8:3, 4
30 Revelation 5:11, 12
31 Revelation 7:9
32 Revelation 21:4
33 Revelation 7:17
34 Ephesians 4:3
35 Psalm 133:1
36 Isaiah 26:3
37 Philippians 3:20

SOME WELL-GUARDED SECRETS--   CHAPTER XI

1 Haggai 1:5, 7
2 Luke 6:38
3 Ibid.
4 II Chronicles 6:18
5 Ibid.
6 See Solomon's Prayer:
   II Chronicles 6:14-42 (NIV)

7 II Chronicles 7:13-14 (NIV)
8 III John v. 2
9 "Prayer May Help, Medical
   Study Finds," Miami Herald
   January 23, 1989, p. 12a.
10 Jeremiah 29:11 (NIV)
11 Ibid., 29:12 (NIV)

[12] Luke 18:13
[13] I John 1:9
[14] Mark 10:5 (NIV)
[15] Mark 10:51
[16] II Kings 20:3
[17] I Thessalonians 5:18
[18] II Corinthians 9:12
[19] Luke 17:17
[20] Philippians 4:6
[21] Psalm 119:62
[22] Psalm 119:164
[23] Matthew 6:16, 17
[24] Ezra 8:22-23
[25] Book of Esther
[26] Deuteronomy 9:18
[27] Psalm 35:13
[28] Psalm 108:24
[29] John 14:13
[30] Malachi 3:10 (NIV)
[31] Luke 6:38
[32] II Chronicles 32:25
[33] James 1:5

[34] Proverbs 4:7
[35] Luke 3:21
[36] Matthew 4:2
[37] Mark 1:35
[38] Luke 5:12-16
[39] Luke 9:18
[40] John 17
[41] Luke 17:41
[42] Matthew 26:39
[43] Mark 14:35
[44] Luke 22:31, 32 (NIV)
[45] Luke 23:34 (NIV)
[46] Mark 16:51
[47] Hebrews 10:25
[48] Ezekiel 22:30
    II Peter 3:7, 10
[49] Genesis 6:11-14
[50] Genesis 6:5
[51] Ezekiel 22:30
[52] I Peter 5:8
[53] Jeremiah 29:11

PRESENT-DAY PRAYER POWER--   CHAPTER XII

[1] Malachi 3:6
[2] Revelation 3:17
[3] Revelation 3:18
[4] Revelation 3:21
[5] Matthew 26:40
[6] Matthew 26:41
[7] Job 14:15
[8] Isaiah 41:21
[9] I Chronicles 4:10
[10] Also, see Christian
    Chronicles April
    1991, p. 2.

[11] Psalm 34:2, 3
[12] Psalm 44:8
[13] I Samuel 1:9-20
[14] Ephesians 3:20
[15] Genesis 2:18-25;
    Matthew 19:3-9
[16] I Corinthians 7:5
[17] Isaiah 26:3
[18] Luke 6:38
[19] James 2:23
[20] Romans 4:11, 12, 16, 18
[21] Matthew 5:16
[22] Acts 2:38

ON EAGLE-S WINGS--   CHAPTER XIII

[1] Psalm 107:26-28
[2] Isaiah 40:31
[3] John 15:11

[4] Isaiah 35:10
[5] I Peter 1:8
[6] John 8:56

[7] Exodus 15:11
[8] Exodus 15:21
[9] I Samuel 2:1-10
[10] Adar corresponds to mid-February to mid-March. J. D. Douglas & Merrill C. Tenney editors, The New International Dictionary (Grand Rapids, Michigan Zondervan Publishing House 1987), p. 15.
[11] Esther 9:22
[12] Nehemiah 8-13
Ezra 3:8-13; 4-10
[13] Luke 1:14
[14] Luke 1:67, 69 (NIV) (for the entire prohecy see verses 67-79)
[15] Luke 1:42, 45
[16] Luke 1:38
[17] Luke 1:46-55
[18] Luke 10:21 (NIV)
[19] Revelation 5:11, 12
[20] Revelation 5:8-10; 8:3, 4
[21] Matthew 25:31-45
[22] Revelation 20:10; 21:8
[23] John 3:5; Acts 2:36-38
[24] Revelation 21:5
[25] Luke 8:13; 15-10
[26] Isaiah 35:1-10